ISBN 978-0-484-40497-6
PIBN 10202543

MANUAL

FOR THE

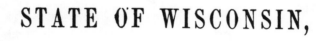

USE OF THE ASSEMBLY,

OF THE

STATE OF WISCONSIN,

FOR THE YEAR 1853.

PREPARED PURSUANT TO A RESOLUTION OF THE ASSEMBLY.

MADISON:
BROWN & CARPENTER, PRINTERS.

1853.

ASSEMBLY MANUAL.

~~~~~~~~~~~~~

CONSTITUTION OF THE STATE OF WISCONSIN.

———

PREAMBLE.

We, the People of Wisconsin, grateful to Almighty God for our freedom, in order to secure its blessings, form a more perfect government, insure domestic tranquillity, and promote the general welfare, do establish this constitution.

ARTICLE I.

DECLARATION OF RIGHTS.

SECTION 1. All men are born equally free and independent, and have certain inherent rights: among these are life, liberty, and the pursuit of happiness. To secure these rights, governments are instituted among men, deriving their just powers from the consent of the governed.

SEC. 2. There shall be neither slavery nor involuntary servitude in this state, otherwise than for the punishment of crime, whereof the party shall have been duly convicted.

SEC. 3. Every person may freely speak, write and publish his sentiments on all subjects, being responsible for the abuse of that right, and no laws shall be passed to restrain or abridge the liberty of speech or of the press. In all criminal prosecutions or indictments for libel, the truth may be given in evidence; and if it shall appear to the jury that the matter charged as libelous be true, and was published with good motives and for justifiable ends, the party shall be acquitted; and the jury shall have the right to determine the law and the fact.

SEC. 4. The right of the people peaceably to assemble to consult for the common good, and to petition the government, or any department thereof, shall never be abridged.

SEC. 5. The right of trial by jury shall remain inviolate; and shall extend to all cases at law, without regard to the amount in controversy; but a jury trial may be waived by the parties in all cases, in the manner prescribed by law.

SEC. 6. Excessive bail shall not be required, nor shall excessive fines be imposed, nor cruel nor unjust punishments inflicted.

SEC. 7. In all criminal prosecutions, the accused shall enjoy the right to be heard by himself and counsel; to demand the nature and cause of the accusations against him; to meet the witness face to face; to have compulsory process to compel the attendance of witnesses in his behalf; and in prosecutions by indictment or information, to a speedy and public trial by an impartial jury of the county or district wherein the offence shall have been committed; which county or district shall have been previously ascertained by law.

SEC. 8. No person shall be held to answer for a criminal offence unless on the presentment or indictment of a grand jury, except in cases of impeachment, or in cases cognizable by justices of the peace, arising in the army or navy, or in the militia when in actual service in time of war or public danger; and no person for the same offence shall be twice put in jeopardy of punishment, nor shall be compelled in any criminal case to be a witness against himself. All persons shall, before conviction, be bailable by sufficient sureties, except for capital offences, when the proof is evident or the presumption great; and the privilege of the writ of habeas corpus shall not be suspended unless when, in cases of rebellion or invasion, the public safety may require.

Sec. 9. Every person is entitled to a certain remedy in the laws, for all injuries or wrongs which he may receive in his person, property, or character; he ought to obtain justice freely, and without being obliged to purchase it; completely and without denial—promptly and without delay, conformably to the laws.

Sec. 10. Treason against the state shall consist only in levying war against the same, or in adhering to its enemies, giving them aid and comfort. No person shall be convicted of treason unless on the testimony of two witnesses to the same overt act, or on confession in open court.

Sec. 11. The right of the people to be secure in their persons, houses, papers, and effects, against unreasonable searches and seizures shall not be violated, and no warrant shall issue but upon probable cause, supported by oath or affirmation, and particularly describing the place to be searched, and the persons or things to be seized.

Sec. 12. No bill of attainder, ex post facto law, nor any law impairing the obligation of contracts, shall ever be passed; and no conviction shall work corruption of blood or forfeiture of estate.

Sec. 13. The property of no person shall be taken for public use without just compensation therefor.

Sec. 14. All lands within the state are declared to be allodial, and feudal tenures are prohibited. Leases and grants of agricultural land, for a longer term than fifteen years, in which rent or service of any kind shall be reserved and all fines and like restraints upon alienation, reserved in any grant of land hereafter made, are declared to be void.

Sec. 15. No distinction shall ever be made by law between resident aliens and citizens, in reference to the possession, enjoyment, or descent of property.

SEC. 16. No person shall be imprisoned for debt arising out of, or founded on a contract, expressed or implied.

SEC. 17. The privilege of the debtor to enjoy the necessary comforts of life, shall be recognized by wholesome laws, exempting a reasonable amount of property from seizure or sale for the payment of any debt or liability hereafter contracted.

SEC. 18. The right of every man to worship Almighty God according to the dictates of his own conscience, shall never be infringed, nor shall any man be compelled to attend, erect, or support any place of worship, or maintain any ministry against his consent. Nor shall any control of, or interference with the rights of conscience be permitted, or any preference be given by law to any religious establishments, or mode of worship. Nor shall any money be drawn from the treasury for the benefit of religious societies, or religious or theological seminaries.

SEC. 19. No religious tests shall ever be required as a qualification for any office of public trust, under the state, and no person shall be rendered incompetent to give evidence in any court of law or equity, in consequence of his opinions on the subject of religion.

SEC. 20. The military shall be in strict subordination to the civil power.

SEC. 21. Writs of error shall never be prohibited by law.

SEC. 22. The blessings of a free government can only be maintained by a firm adherence to justice, moderation, temperance, frugality, and virtue, and by frequent recurrence to fundamental principles.

ARTICLE II.

BOUNDARIES.

SECTION 1. It is hereby ordained and declared that the state of Wisconsin doth consent and accept of the boundaries prescribed in the act of congress entitled " an act to enable the people of Wisconsin territory to form a constitution and state government, and for the admission of such state into the Union," approved August sixth, one thousand eight hundred and forty six, to wit: Beginning at the north-east corner of the state of Illinois, that is to say, at a point in the centre of Lake Michigan, where the line of forty-two degrees and thirty minutes of north latitude crosses the same; thence running with the boundary line of the state of Michigan, through Lake Michigan, Green Bay, to the mouth of the Menomonee river; thence up the channel of the said river to the Brule river; thence up said last mentioned river to Lake Brule; thence along the southern shore of Lake Brule, in a direct line to the centre of the channel between Middle and South islands, in the Lake of the Desert; thence in a direct line to the head waters of the Montreal river, as marked upon the survey made by captain Cram; thence down the main channel of the Montreal river to the middle of Lake Superior; thence through the centre of Lake Superior to the mouth of the St. Louis river; thence up the main channel of said river to the first rapids in the same, above the Indian village, according to Nicollet's map; thence due south to the main branch of the river St. Croix; thence down the main channel of said river to the Mississippi; thence down the centre of the main channel of that river to the north-west corner of the state of Illinois; thence due east with the northern boundary of the state of Illinois, to the place of beginning, as established by "an act to enable the people of the Illinois territory to form a constitution and state government, and for the admission of such state into the Union on an equal footing with the original states," approved April 18th, 1818. [*Provided however, That the following alteration of the aforesaid boundary be, and hereby is, proposed to the congress of the United States as the preference of the state of Wisconsin, and if the same shall be assented and agreed to by the congress of the United States, then the same shall be, and forever remain obligatory on the state of Wisconsin, viz.: leaving the aforesaid boundary line at the foot of the rapids of the St. Louis river; thence in a direct line, bearing south-

* Not assented to by Congress.

2

westerly, to the mouth of the Iskodewabo, or Rum river, where the same empties into the Mississippi river; thence down the main channel of the said Mississippi river, as prescribed in the aforesaid boundary.]

SEC. 2. The propositions contained in the act of congress, are hereby accepted, ratified and confirmed, and shall remain irrevocable without the consent of the United States, and it is hereby ordained that this state shall never interfere with the primary disposal of the soil within the same by the United States; nor with any regulations congress may find necessary for securing the title in such soil to bona fide purchasers thereof; and no tax shall be imposed on land, the property of the United States; and in no case shall non-resident proprietors be taxed higher than residents. Provided, That nothing in this constitution, or in the act of congress aforesaid, shall in any manner prejudice or affect the right of the state of Wisconsin to five hundred thousand acres of land granted to said state, and to be hereafter selected and located, by, and under the act of congress, entitled "an act to appropriate the proceeds of the sales of the public lands, and grant pre-emption rights," approved September 4th, 1841.

ARTICLE III.

SUFFRAGE.

SECTION 1. Every male person, of the age of twenty-one years or upwards, belonging to either of the following classes, who shall have resided in the state for one year next preceding any election, shall be deemed a qualified elector at such election:

1. White citizens of the United States.

2. White persons of foreign birth, who shall have declared their intention to become citizens, conformably to the laws of the United States on the subject of naturalization.

3. Persons of Indian blood, who have once been declared by law of congress to be citizens of the United States, any subsequent law of congress to the contrary notwithstanding.

4. Civilized persons of Indian descent, not members of any tribe. Provided, That the legislature may at any time, extend by law, the right of suffrage to persons not herein enumerated; but no such law shall be in force until the same shall have been submitted to a vote of the people at a general election, and approved by a majority of all the votes cast at such election.

SEC. 2. No person under guardianship, non compos mentis, or insane, shall be qualified to vote at any election; nor shall any person convicted of treason or felony be qualified to vote at any election unless restored to civil rights.

SEC. 3. All votes shall be given by ballot, except for such township officers as may by law be directed or allowed to be otherwise chosen.

SEC. 4. No person shall be deemed to have lost his residence in this state by reason of his absence on business of the United States, or of this state.

SEC. 5. No soldier, seaman or marine, in the army or navy of the United States, shall be deemed a resident of this state in consequence of being stationed within the same.

SEC. 6. Laws may be passed excluding from the right of suffrage all persons who have been or may be convicted of bribery or larceny, or of any infamous crime, and depriving every person who shall make, or become directly or indirectly interested in any bet or wager depending upon the result of any election, from the right to vote at such election.

ARTICLE IV.

LEGISLATIVE.

SECTION 1. The legislative power shall be vested in a senate and assembly.

SEC. 2. The number of the members of the assembly shall never be less than fifty-four, nor more than one hundred. The senate shall consist of a number not more than one-third, nor less than one-fourth of the number of the members of the assembly.

Sec. 3. The legislature shall provide by law for an enumeration of the inhabitants of the state, in the year one thousand eight hundred and fifty-five, and at the end of every ten years thereafter; and at their first session after such enumeration, and also after each enumeration made by the authority of the United States, the legislature shall apportion and district anew the members of the senate and assembly, according to the number of inhabitants, excluding Indians not taxed, and soldiers and officers of the United States army and navy.

Sec. 4. The members of the assembly shall be chosen annually by single districts, on the Tuesday succeeding the first Monday of November, by the qualified electors of the several districts; such districts to be bounded by county, precinct, town or ward lines, to consist of contiguous territory, and be in as compact form as practicable.

Sec. 5. The senators shall be chosen by single districts of convenient contiguous territory, at the same time and in the same manner as members of the assembly are required to be chosen, and no assembly district shall be divided in the formation of a senate district. The senate districts shall be numbered in regular series, and the senators chosen by the odd numbered districts shall go out of office at the expiration of the first year, and 'the senators chosen by the even numbered districts shall go out of office at the expiration of the second year, and thereafter the senators shall be chosen for the term of two years.

Sec. 6. No person shall be eligible to the legislature who shall not have resided one year within the state, and be a qualified elector in the district which he may be chosen to represent.

Sec. 7. Each house shall be the judge of the elections, returns and qualifications of its own members, and a majority of each shall constitute a quorum to do business; but a smaller number may adjourn from day to day, and may compel the attendance of absent members, in such manner and under such penalties as each house may provide.

SEC. 8. Each house may determine the rules of its own proceedings, punish for contempt and disorderly behavior, and, with the concurrence of two-thirds of all the members elected, expel a member; but no member shall be expelled a second time for the same cause.

SEC. 9. Each house shall choose its own officers, and the senate shall choose a temporary president, when the lieutenant-governor shall not attend as president, or shall act as governor.

SEC. 10. Each house shall keep a journal of its proceedings, and publish the same, except such parts as require secrecy. The doors of each house shall be kept open except when the public welfare shall require secrecy. Neither house shall, without the consent of the other, adjourn for more than three days.

SEC. 11. The legislature shall meet at the seat of government, at such time as shall be provided by law, once in each year, and not oftener, unless convened by the governor.

SEC. 12. No member of the legislature shall, during the term for which he was elected, be appointed or elected to any civil office in the state, which shall have been created, or the emoluments of which shall have been increased, during the term for which he was elected.

SEC. 13. No person being a member of congress, or holding any military or civil office under the United States, shall be eligible to a seat in the legislature; and if any person shall, after his election as a member of the legislature, be elected to congress, or be appointed to any office, civil or military, under the government of the United States, his acceptance thereof shall vacate his seat.

SEC. 14. The governor shall issue writs of election to fill such vacancies as may occur in either house of the legislature.

SEC. 15. Members of the legislature shall, in all cases except treason, felony and breach of the peace, be privileged from arrest; nor shall they be subject to any civil process, during the session of the legislature, nor for fifteen days next before the commencement and after the termination of each session.

SEC. 16. No member of the legislature shall be liable in any civil action or criminal prosecution whatever, for words spoken in debate.

SEC. 17. The style of the laws of the state shall be, "The people of the state of Wisconsin, represented in senate and assembly, do enact as follows :" and no law shall be enacted except by bill.

SEC. 18. No private or local bill, which may be passed by the legislature, shall embrace more than one subject, and that shall be expressed in the title.

SEC. 19. Any bill may originate in either house of the legislature ; and a bill passed by one house may be amended by the other.

SEC. 20. The yeas and nays of the members of either house, on any question, shall, at the request of one-sixth of those present, be entered on the journal.

SEC. 21. Each member of the legislature shall receive for his services, two dollars and fifty cents for each day's attendance during the session, and ten cents for every mile he shall travel in going to and returning from the place of the meeting of the legislature, on the most usual route.

SEC. 22. The legislature may confer upon the boards of supervisors of the several counties of the state, such powers, of a local, legislative, and administrative character as they shall from time to time prescribe.

SEC. 23. The legislature shall establish but one system of town and county government, which shall be as nearly uniform as practicable.

SEC. 24. The legislature shall never authorize any lottery, or grant any divorce.

SEC. 25. The legislature shall provide by law that all stationery required for the use of the state, and all printing authorized and required by them to be done for their use, or for the state, shall be let by contract to the lowest bidder; but the legislature may establish a maximum price. No member of the legislature, or other state officer, shall be interested either directly or indirectly, in any such contract.

SEC. 26. The legislature shall never grant any extra compensation to any public officer, agent, servant, or contractor, after the services shall have been rendered, or the contract entered into. Nor shall the compensation of any public officer be increased or diminished during his term of office.

SEC. 27. The legislature shall direct by law in what manner and in what courts suits may be brought against the state.

SEC. 28. Members of the legislature, and all officers, executive and judicial, except such inferior officers as may be by law exempted, shall, before they enter upon the duties of their respective offices, take and subscribe an oath or affirmation to support the constitution of the United States, and the constitution of the state of Wisconsin, and faithfully to discharge the duties of their respective offices to the best of their ability.

SEC. 29. The legislature shall determine what persons shall constitute the militia of the state, and may provide for organizing and disciplining the same, in such manner as shall be prescribed by law.

SEC. 30. In all elections to be made by the legislature, the members thereof shall vote *viva voce*, and their votes shall be entered on the journal.

ARTICLE V.

EXECUTIVE.

SECTION 1. The executive power shall be vested in a governor, who shall hold his office for two years. A lieutenant governor shall be elected at the same time, and for the same term.

SEC. 2. No person, except a citizen of the United States, and a qualified elector of the state, shall be eligible to the office of governor or lieutenant governor.

SEC. 3. The governor and lieutenant governor shall be elected by the qualified electors of the state, at the times and places of choosing members of the legislature. The persons respectively having the highest number of votes for governor and lieutenant governor shall be elected. But in case two or more shall have an equal and the highest number of votes for governor or lieutenant governor, the two houses of the legislature, at its next annual session, shall forthwith, by joint ballot, choose one of the persons so having an equal and the highest number of votes for governor or lieutenant governor. The returns of·election for governor and lieutenant governor shall be made in such manner as shall be provided by law.

SEC. 4. The governor shall be commander-in-chief of the military and naval forces of the state. He shall have power to convene the legislature on extraordinary occasions; and in case of invasion, or danger from the prevalence of contagious disease at the seat of government, he may convene them at any other suitable place within the state. He shall communicate to the legislature, at every session, the condition of the state, and recommend such matters to them for their consideration, as he may deem expedient. He shall transact all necessary business with the officers of the government, civil and military. He shall expedite all such measures as may be resolved upon by the legislature, and shall take care that the laws be faithfully executed.

SEC. 5. The governor shall receive, during his continuance in office, an annual compensation of one thousand two hundred and fifty dollars.

SEC. 6. The governor shall have power to grant reprieves, commutations, and pardons, after conviction, for all offences, except treason and cases of impeachment, upon such conditions, and with such restrictions and limitations as he may think proper,·subject to such regulations as may be provided by law relative to the manner of applying for pardons. Upon conviction for treason, he shall have the power to suspend the execution of the sentence until the case shall be reported to the legislature, at its next meeting, when the legislature shall either pardon, or commute the sentence, direct the execution of the sentence, or grant a further reprieve. He shall annually communicate to the legislature each case of reprieve, commutation, or pardon granted, stating the name of the convict, the crime of which he was convicted, the sentence and its date, and the date of the commutation, pardon, or reprieve, with his reasons for granting the same.

SEC. 7. In case of the impeachment of the governor, or his removal from office, death, inability from mental or physical disease, resignation, or absence from the state, the powers and duties of the office shall devolve upon the lieutenant governor for the residue of the term, or until the governor, absent or impeached, shall have returned, or the disability shall cease. But when the governor shall, with the consent of the legislature, be out of the state in time of war, at the head of the military force thereof, he shall continue commander-in-chief of the military force of the state.

SEC. 8. The lieutenant governor shall be president of the senate, but shall have only a casting vote therein. If during a vacancy in the office of governor, the lieutenant governor shall be impeached, displaced, resign, die, or from mental or physical disease become incapable of performing the duties of his office, or be absent from the state, the secretary of state shall act as governor until the vacancy shall be filled, or the disability shall cease.

SEC. 9. The lieutenant governor shall receive double the per diem allowance of members of the senate, for every day's attendance as president of the senate, and the same mileage as shall be allowed to members of the legislature.

SEC. 10. Every bill which shall have passed the legislature shall, before it becomes a law, be presented to the governor. If he approve, he shall sign it; but if not, he shall return it, with his objections, to that house in which it shall have originated, who shall enter the objections at large upon the journal, and proceed to reconsider it. If, after such reconsideration, two-thirds of the members present shall agree to pass the bill, it shall be sent, together with the objections, to the other house, by which it shall likewise be reconsidered, and if approved by two-thirds of the members present, it shall become a law. But in all such cases, the votes of both houses shall be determined by yeas and nays, and the names of the members voting for or against the bill shall be entered on the journal of each house respectively. If any bill shall not be returned by the governor within three days (Sundays excepted) after it shall have been presented to him, the same shall be a law, unless the legislature shall, by their adjournment, prevent its return; in which case it shall not be a law.

ARTICLE VI.

ADMINISTRATIVE.

SECTION 1. There shall be chosen by the qualified electors of the state, at the times and places of choosing the members of the legislature, a secretary of state, treasurer, and an attorney general, who shall severally hold their offices for the term of two years.

SEC. 2. The secretary of state shall keep a fair record of the official acts of the legislature and executive department of the state, and shall, when required, lay the same and all matters relative thereto before either branch of the legislature. He shall be *ex-officio* auditor, and shall perform such other duties as shall be assigned him by law. He shall receive as a compensation for his services, yearly, such sum as shall be provided by law, and shall keep his office at the seat of government.

SEC. 3. The powers, duties, and compensation of the treasurer and attorney general shall be prescribed by law.

SEC. 4. Sheriffs, coroners, registers of deeds, and district attorneys shall be chosen by the electors of the respective counties, once in every two years, and as often as vacancies shall happen. Sheriffs shall hold no other office, and be ineligible for two years next succeeding the termination of their offices. They may be required by law to renew their security from time to time; and in default of giving such new security, their offices shall be deemed vacant. But the county shall never be made responsible for the acts of the sheriff. The governor may remove any officer in this section mentioned, giving to such officer a copy of the charges against him, and an opportunity of being heard in his defence.

ARTICLE VII.

JUDICIARY.

SECTION 1. The court for the trial of impeachments shall be composed of the senate. The house of representatives shall have the power of impeaching all civil officers of this state, for corrupt conduct in office, or for crimes and misdemeanors; but a majority of all the members elected shall concur in an impeachment. On the trial of an impeachment against the governor, the lieutenant governor shall not act as a member of the court. No judicial officer shall exercise his office after he shall have been impeached, until his acquittal. Before the trial of an impeachment, the members of the court shall take an oath or affirmation truly and impartially to try the impeachment, according to evidence; and no person shall be convicted without the concurrence of two-thirds of the members present. Judgment in cases of impeachment shall not extend further than to removal from office, or removal from office and disqualification to hold any office of honor, profit, or trust, under the state; but the party impeached shall be liable to indictment, trial and punishment, according to law

SEC. 2. The judicial power of this state, both as to matters of law and equity, shall be vested in a supreme court, circuit courts, courts of probate, and in justices of the peace. The legislature may also vest such jurisdiction as shall be deemed necessary in municipal courts, and shall have power to establish inferior courts in the several counties, with limited civil and criminal jurisdiction: Provided, That the jurisdiction which may be vested in municipal courts shall not exceed, in their respective municipalities, that of circuit courts in their respective circuits, as prescribed in this constitution; and that the legislature shall provide as well for the election of judges of the municipal courts as of the judges of inferior courts, by the qualified electors of the respective jurisdictions: The term of office of the judges of the said municipal and inferior courts shall not be longer than that of the judges of the circuit courts.

SEC. 3. The supreme court, except in cases otherwise provided in this constitution, shall have appellate jurisdiction only, which shall be co-extensive with the state; but in no case removed to the supreme court, shall a trial by jury be allowed. The supreme court shall have a general superintending control over all inferior courts; it shall have power to issue writs of habeas corpus, manda- mus, injunction, quo warranto, certiorari, and other original and remedial writs, and to hear and determine the same.

SEC. 4. For the term of five years, and thereafter until the legis- lature shall otherwise provide, the judges of the several circuit courts shall be judges of the supreme court, four of whom shall constitute a quorum, and the concurrence of a majority of the judges present shall be necessary to a decision. The legislature shall have power, if they should think it expedient and necessary, to provide by law, for the organization of a separate supreme court, with the jurisdiction and powers prescribed in this constitution, to consist of one chief justice and two associate justices, to be elected by the qualified electors of the state, at such time and in such manner as the legislature may provide. The separate supreme court, when so organized, shall not be changed or discontinued by the legislature; the judges thereof shall be so classified that but one of them shall go out of office at the same time, and their term of office shall be the same as is provided for the judges of the cir- cuit court. And whenever the legislature may consider it necessary to establish a separate supreme court, they shall have power to reduce the number of circuit judges to four, and subdivide the judicial circuits, but no such subdivision or reduction shall take effect until after the expiration of the term of some one of the said judges, or until a vacancy occur by some other means.

SEC. 5. The state shall be divided into five judicial circuits, to be composed as follows: The first circuit shall comprise the coun- ties of Racine, Walworth, Rock and Green. The second circuit, the counties of Milwaukee, Waukesha, Jefferson and Dane. The third circuit, the counties of Washington, Dodge, Columbia, Mar- quette, Sauk and Portage. The fourth circuit, the counties of

Brown, Manitowoc, Sheboygan, Fond du Lac, Winnebago and Calumet. And the fifth circuit shall comprise the counties of Iowa, Lafayette, Grant, Crawford and St. Croix; and the county of Richland shall be attached to Iowa, the county of Chippewa to the county of Crawford, and the county of La Pointe to the county of. St. Croix, for judicial purposes, until otherwise provided by the legislature.

Sec. 6. The legislature may alter the limits, or increase the number of circuits, making them as compact and convenient as practicable, and bounding them by county lines, but no such alteration or increase shall have the effect to remove a judge from office. In case of an increase of circuits, the judge or judges shall be elected as provided in this constitution, and receive a salary not less than that herein provided for judges of the circuit court.

Sec. 7. For each circuit there shall be a judge chosen by the qualified electors therein, who shall hold his office as is provided in this constitution, and until his successor shall be chosen and qualified; and after he shall have been elected, he shall reside in the circuit for which he was elected. One of said judges shall be designated as chief justice, in such manner as the legislature shall provide. And the legislature shall, at its first session, provide by law, as well for the election of, as for classifying the judges of the circuit court, to be elected under this constitution in such manner that one of said judges shall go out of office in two years, one in three years, one in four years, one in five years, and one in six years, and thereafter the judge elected to fill the office, shall hold the same for six years.

Sec. 8. The circuit courts shall have original jurisdiction in all matters, civil and criminal, within this state, not excepted in this constitution, and not hereafter prohibited by law, and appellate jurisdiction from all inferior courts and tribunals, and a supervisory control over the same. They shall also have power to issue writs of habeas corpus, mandamus, injunction, quo warranto, certiorari, and all other writs necessary to carry into effect their orders, judgments and decrees, and give them a general control over inferior courts and jurisdictions.

Sec. 9. When a vacancy shall happen in the office of judge of the supreme or circuit courts, such vacancy shall be filled by an appointment of the Governor, which shall continue until a successor is elected and qualified; and when elected, such successor shall hold his office the residue of the unexpired term. There shall be no election for a judge or judges at any general election for state or county officers, nor within thirty days either before or after such election.

Sec. 10 Each of the judges of the supreme and circuit courts shall receive a salary, payable quarterly, of not less than one thousand five hundred dollars annually; they shall receive no fees of office, or other compensation than their salaries; they shall hold no office of public trust, except a judicial office, during the term for which they are respectively elected, and all votes for either of them, for any office except a judicial office, given by the legislature or the people, shall be void. No person shall be eligible to the office of judge, who shall not, at the time of his election, be a citizen of the United States, and have attained the age of twenty-five years, and be a qualified elector within the jurisdiction for which he may be chosen.

Sec. 11. The supreme court shall hold at least one term annually, at the seat of government of the state, at such time as shall be provided by law, and the legislature may provide for holding other terms, and at other places, when they may deem it necessary. A circuit court shall be held at least twice in each year, in each county of this state, organized for judicial purposes. The judges of the circuit court may hold courts for each other, and shall do so when required by law.

Sec. 12. There shall be a clerk of the circuit court chosen in each county organized for judicial purposes, by the qualified electors thereof, who shall hold his office for two years, subject to removal, as shall be provided by law. In case of a vacancy, the judge of the circuit court shall have the power to appoint a clerk, until the vacancy shall be filled by an election. The clerk thus elected or appointed, shall give such security as the legislature may require; and when elected, shall hold his office for a full term. The supreme court shall appoint its own clerk, and the clerk of a circuit court may be appointed clerk of the supreme court.

Sec. 13. Any judge of the supreme or circuit court may be removed from office by address of both houses of the 'legislature, if two-thirds of all the members elected to each house concur therein, but no removal shall be made by virtue of this section, unless the judge complained of shall have been served with a copy of the charges against him, as the ground of address, and shall have had an opportunity of being heard in his defence. On the question of removal, the ayes and noes shall be entered on the journals.

Sec. 14. There shall be chosen in each county, by the qualified electors thereof, a judge of probate, who shall hold his office for two years, and until his successor shall be elected and qualified, and whose jurisdiction, powers and duties, shall be prescribed by law : Provided, however, That the legislature shall have power to abolish the office of judge of probate in any county, and to confer probate powers upon such inferior courts as may be established in said county.

Sec. 15. The electors of the several towns, at their annual town meetings, and the electors of cities and villages, at their charter elections, shall in such manner as the legislature may direct, elect justices of the peace, whose term of office shall be for two years, and until their successors in office shall be elected and qualified. In case of an election to fill a vacancy occurring before the expiration of a full term, the justice elected shall hold for the residue of the unexpired term. Their number and classification shall be regulated by law. And the tenure of two years shall in no wise interfere with the classification in the first instance. The justices thus elected shall have such civil and criminal jurisdiction as shall be prescribed by law.

Sec. 16. The legislature shall pass laws for the regulation of tribunals of conciliation, defining their powers and duties. Such tribunals may be established in and for any township, and shall have power to render judgment, to be obligatory on the parties, when they shall voluntarily submit their matter in difference to arbitration, and agree to abide the judgment, or assent thereto in writing.

SEC. 17. The style of all writs and process shall be, "The state of Wisconsin." All criminal prosecutions shall be carried on in the name and by the authority of the same; and all indictments shall conclude against the peace and dignity of the state.

SEC. 18 The legislature shall impose a tax on all civil suits commenced or prosecuted in the municipal, inferior, or circuit courts, which shall constitute a fund to be applied toward the payment of the salary of judges.

SEC. 19. The testimony in causes in equity, shall be taken in like manner as in cases at law; and the office of master in chancery is hereby prohibited.

SEC. 20. Any suitor in any court of this state, shall have the right to prosecute or defend his suit either in his own proper person or by an attorney or agent of his choice.

SEC. 21. The legislature shall provide by law for the speedy publication of all statute laws, and of such judicial decisions made within the state, as may be deemed expedient. And no general law shall be in force until published.

SEC. 22. The legislature at its first session after the adoption of this constitution, shall provide for the appointment of three commissioners, whose duty shall be to inquire into, revise and simplify the rules of practice, pleadings, forms, and proceedings, and arrange a system adapted to the courts of record of this state, and report the same to the legislature, subject to their modification and adoption; and such commission shall terminate upon the rendering of the report, unless otherwise provided by law.

SEC. 23. The legislature may provide for the appointment of one or more persons in each organized county, and may vest in such persons such judicial powers as shall be prescribed by law:

Provided, That said power shall not exceed that of a judge of the circuit court at chambers.

ARTICLE VIII.

FINANCE.

SECTION 1. The rule of taxation shall be uniform, and taxes shall be levied upon such property as the legislature shall prescribe.

SEC. 2. No money shall be paid out of the treasury, except in pursuance of an appropriation by law.

SEC. 3. The credit of the state shall never be given or loaned in aid of any individual, association, or corporation.

SEC. 4. The state shall never contract any public debt, except in the cases and manner herein provided.

SEC. 5. The legislature shall provide for an annual tax sufficient to defray the estimated expenses of the state for each year; and whenever the expenses of any year shall exceed the income, the legislature shall provide for levying a tax for the ensuing year, sufficient, with other sources of income, to pay the deficiency, as well as the estimated expenses of such ensuing year.

SEC. 6. For the purpose of defraying extraordinary expenditures, the state may contract public debts; but such debt shall never in the aggregate exceed one hundred thousand dollars. Every such debt shall be authorized by law, for some purpose or purposes to be distinctly specified therein; and the vote of a majority of all the members elected to each house, to be taken by yeas and nays, shall be necessary to the passage of such law; and every such law shall provide for levying an annual tax sufficient to pay the annual interest of such debt, and the principal within five years from the passage of such law, and shall specially appropriate the proceeds of such taxes to the payment of such principal and interest; and such appropriation shall not be repealed, nor the taxes be postponed or diminished until the principal and interest of such debt shall have been wholly paid.

4

SEC. 7. The legislature may also borrow money to repel invasion, suppress insurrection, or defend the state in time of war; but the money thus raised shall be applied exclusively to the object for which the loan was authorized, or to the repayment of the debt thereby created.

SEC. 8. On the passage in either house of the legislature, of any law which imposes, continues, or renews a tax, or creates a debt or charge, or makes, continues, or renews an appropriation of public or trust money, or releases, discharges, or commutes a claim or demand of the state, the question shall be taken by yeas and nays, which shall be duly entered on the journal; and three-fifths of all the members elected to such house, shall in all such cases be required to constitute a quorum therein.

SEC. 9. No scrip, certificate, or other evidence of state debt whatsoever, shall be issued, except for such debts as are authorized by the sixth and seventh sections of this article.

SEC. 10. The state shall never contract any debt for works of internal improvement, or be a party in carrying on such works; but whenever grants of land, or other property, shall have been made to the state, especially dedicated by the grant to particular works of internal improvement, the state may carry on such particular works, and shall devote thereto the avails of such grants, and may pledge or appropriate the revenues derived from such works in aid of their completion.

ARTICLE IX.

EMINENT DOMAIN AND PROPERTY OF THE STATE.

SECTION 1. The state shall have concurrent jurisdiction on all rivers and lakes bordering on this state, so far as such rivers or lakes shall form a common boundary to the state, and any other state or territory now or hereafter to be formed and bounded by the same. And the river Mississippi, and the navigable waters leading into the Mississippi and St. Lawrence, and the carrying places between the same, shall be common highways, and forever free, as well to the inhabitants of the state as to the citizens of the United States, without any tax, impost, or duty therefor.

SEC. 2. The title to all lands, and other property, which have accrued to the territory of Wisconsin, by grant, gift, purchase, forfeiture, escheat, or otherwise, shall vest in the state of Wisconsin.

SEC. 3. The people of the state, in their right of sovereignty, are declared to possess the ultimate property in and to all lands within the jurisdiction of the state; and all lands, the title to which shall fail from a defect of heirs, shall revert, or escheat to the people.

ARTICLE X.

EDUCATION.

SECTION 1. The supervision of public instruction shall be vested in a state superintendent, and such other officers as the legislature shall direct. The state superintendent shall be chosen by the qualified electors of the state, in such manner as the legislature shall provide; his powers, duties and compensation shall be prescribed by law: Provided, That his compensation shall not exceed the sum of twelve hundred dollars annually.

SEC. 2. The proceeds of all lands that have been or hereafter may be granted by the United States to this state, for educational purposes, (except the lands heretofore granted for the purposes of a university,) and all moneys, and the clear proceeds of all property, that may accrue to the state by forfeiture or escheat, and all moneys which may be paid as an equivalent for exemption from military duty, and the clear proceeds of all fines collected in the several counties for any breach of the penal laws, and all moneys arising from any grant to the state, where the purposes of such grant are not specified, and the five hundred thousand acres of land to which the state is entitled by the provisions of an act of congress, entitled "an act to appropriate the proceeds of the sales of the public lands, and to grant pre-emption rights," approved the fourth day of September, one thousand eight hundred and forty-one, and also the five per centum of the nett proceeds of the public lands to which the state shall become entitled on her admission into the union, (if congress shall consent to such appropriation of the two grants last mentioned,) shall be set apart as a separate fund, to be called the school fund, the interest of which, and all other revenues derived from the school lands, shall be exclusively applied to the following objects, to wit:

1. To the support and maintenance of common schools in each school district, and the purchase of suitable libraries and apparatus therefor.

2. The residue shall be appropriated to the support and maintenance of academies and normal schools, and suitable libraries and apparatus therefor.

SEC. 3. The legislature shall provide by law for the establishment of district schools, which shall be as nearly uniform as practicable, and such schools shall be free and without charge for tuition to all children between the ages of four and twenty years, and no sectarian instruction shall be allowed therein.

SEC. 4. Each town and city shall be required to raise, by tax, annually, for the support of common schools therein, a sum not less than one-half the amount received by such town or city respectively for school purposes, from the income of the school fund.

SEC. 5. Provision shall be made by law for the distribution of the income of the school fund among the several towns and cities of the state, for the support of common schools therein, in some just proportion to the number of children and youth resident therein, between the ages of four and twenty years, and no appropriation shall be made from the school fund to any city or town, for the year in which said city or town shall fail to raise such tax, nor to any school district for the year in which a school shall not be maintained at least three months.

SEC. 6. Provision shall be made by law for the establishment of a state university, at or near the seat of state government, and for connecting with the same from time to time such colleges in different parts of the state, as the interests of education may require. The proceeds of all lands that have been or may hereafter be granted by the United States to the state for the support of a university, shall be and remain a perpetual fund, to be called the " university fund," the interest of which shall be appropriated to the support of the state university, and no sectarian instruction shall be allowed in such university.

SEC. 7. The secretary of state, treasurer, and attorney general shall constitute a board of commissioners for the sale of the school and university lands, and for the investment of the funds arising therefrom. Any two of said commissioners shall be a quorum for the transaction of all business pertaining to the duties of their office.

SEC. 8. Provision shall be made by law for the sale of all school and university lands, after they shall have been appraised, and when any portion of such lands shall be sold, and the purchase money shall not be paid at the time of the sale, the commissioners shall take security by mortage upon the land sold for the sum remaining unpaid, with seven per cent. interest thereon, payable annually at the office of the treasurer. The commissioners shall be authorized to execute a good and sufficient conveyance to all purchasers of such lands, and to discharge any mortgages taken as security, when the sum due thereon shall have been paid. The commissioners shall have the power to withhold from sale any portion of such lands when they shall deem it expedient, and shall invest all moneys arising from the sale of such lands, as well as all other university and school funds, in such manner as the legislature shall provide, and shall give such security for the faithful performance of their duties as may be required by law.

ARTICLE XI.

CORPORATIONS.

SECTION 1. Corporations without banking powers or privileges may be formed under general laws, but shall not be created by special act, except for municipal purposes, and in cases where, in the judgment of the legislature, the objects of the corporation cannot be attained under general laws. All general laws or special acts enacted under the provisions of this section, may be altered or repealed by the legislature at any time after their passage.

SEC. 2. No municipal corporation shall take private property for public use against the consent of the owner, without the necessity thereof being first established by the verdict of a jury.

SEC. 3. It shall be the duty of the legislature, and they are hereby empowered to provide for the organization of cities and incorporated villages, and to restrict their power of taxation, assessment, borrowing money, contracting debts, and loaning their credit, so as to prevent abuses in assessments and taxation, and in contracting debts by such municipal corporations.

SEC. 4. The legislature shall not have power to create, authorize, or incorporate, by any general or special law, any bank or banking power, or privilege, or any institution or corporation, having any banking power or privilege whatever, except as provided in this article.

SEC. 5. The legislature may submit to the voters at any general election, the question of "bank or no bank," and if at any such election, a number of votes equal to a majority of all the votes cast at such election on that subject shall be in favor of banks, then the legislature shall have power to grant bank charters, or to pass a general banking law, with such restrictions and under such regulations as they may deem expedient and proper for the security of the bill holders: Provided, That no such grant or law shall have any force or effect until the same shall have been submitted to a vote of the electors of the state at some general election, and been approved by a majority of the votes cast on that subject at such election.

ARTICLE XII.

AMENDMENTS.

SECTION 1. Any amendment or amendments to this constitution may be proposed in either house of the legislature, and if the same shall be agreed to by a majority of the members elected to each of the two houses, such proposed amendment or amendments shall be entered on their journals with the yeas and nays taken thereon, and referred to the legislature to be chosen at the next general election, and shall be published for three months previous to the time of holding such election. And if the legislature so next chosen, such proposed amendment or amendments shall be agreed to by a majority of all the members elected to each house, then it shall be the duty of the legislature to submit such proposed amendment or amendments to the people, in such manner and at such time as the legislature shall prescribe, and if the people shall approve and ratify such amendment or amendments by a majority of the electors voting thereon, such amendment or amendments shall become part of the constitution: Provided, That if more than one amendment be submited, they shall be submitted in such manner that the people may vote for or against such amendments separately.

SEC. 2. If at any time a majority of the senate and assembly shall deem it necessary to call a convention to revise or change this constitution, they shall recommend to the electors to vote for or against a convention at the next election for members of the legislature; and if it shall appear that a majority of the electors voting thereon have voted for a convention, the legislature shall at its next session provide for calling such convention.

ARTICLE XIII.

MISCELLANEOUS PROVISIONS.

SECTION 1. The political year for the state of Wisconsin shall commence on the first Monday in January in each year, and the general election shall be holden on the Tuesday succeeding the first Monday in November in each year.

SEC. 2. Any inhabitant of this state who may hereafter be engaged, either directly or indirectly, in a duel, either as principal or accessory, shall forever be disqualified as an elector, and from holding any office under the constitution and laws of this state, and may be punished in such other manner as shall be prescribed by law.

Sec. 3. No member of congress, nor any person holding any office of profit or trust under the United States, (postmasters excepted,) or under any foreign power; no person convicted of any infamous crime in any court within the United States, and no person being a defaulter to the United States, or to this state, or to any county or town therein, or to any state or territory within the United States, shall be eligible to any office of trust, profit, or honor, in this state.

Sec. 4. It shall be the duty of the legislature to provide a great seal for the state, which shall be kept by the secretary of state; and all official acts of the governor, his approbation of the laws excepted, shall be thereby authenticated.

Sec. 5. All persons residing upon Indian lands within any county of the state, and qualified to exercise the right of suffrage under this constitution, shall be entitled to vote at the polls which may be held nearest their residence, for state, United States, or county officers: Provided, that no person shall vote for county officers out of the county in which he resides.

Sec. 6. The elective officers of the legislature, other than the presiding officers, shall be a chief clerk, and a sergeant-at-arms, to be elected by each house.

Sec. 7. No county with an area of nine hundred square miles or less, shall be divided, or have any part stricken therefrom, without submitting the question to a vote of the people of the county, nor unless a majority of all the legal voters of the county voting on the question, shall vote for the same.

Sec. 8. No county seat shall be removed until the point to which it is proposed to be removed, shall be fixed by law, and a majority of the voters of the county, voting on the question, shall have voted in favor of its removal to such point.

Sec. 9. All county officers whose election or appointment is not provided for by this constitution, shall be elected by the electors of the respective counties, or appointed by the boards of supervisors, or other county authorities, as the legislature shall direct. All city, town and village officers, whose election or appointment is not provided for by this constitution, shall be elected by the electors of such cities, towns and villages, or of some division thereof, or appointed by such authorities thereof, as the legislature shall designate for that purpose. All other officers whose election or appointment is not provided for by this constitution, and all officers whose offices may hereafter be created by law, shall be elected by the people, or appointed as the legislature may direct.

SEC. 10. The legislature may declare the cases in which any office shall be deemed vacant, and also the manner of filling the vacancy where no provision is made for that purpose, in this constitution.

ARTICLE XIV.

SCHEDULE.

SECTION 1. That no inconvenience may arise by reason of a change from a territorial to a permanent state government, it is declared that all rights, actions, prosecutions, judgments, claims and contracts, as well of individuals as of bodies corporate, shall continue as if no such change had taken place, and all process which may be issued under the authority of the territory of Wisconsin, previous to its admission into the union of the United States, shall be as valid as if issued in the name of the state.

SEC. 2. All laws now in force in the territory of Wisconsin, which are not repugnant to this constitution, shall remain in force until they expire by their own limitation, or be altered or repealed by the legislature.

SEC. 3. All fines, penalties or forfeitures, accruing to the territory of Wisconsin, shall enure to the use of the state.

SEC. 4. All recognizances heretofore taken, or which may be taken before the change from territorial to a permanent state government, shall remain valid, and shall pass to and may be prosecuted in the name of the state; and all bonds executed to the governor of the territory, or to any other officer or court, in his or

5

their official capacity, shall pass to the governor or state authority, and their successors in office, for the uses therein respectively expressed, and may be sued for and recovered accordingly; and all the estate or property, real, personal or mixed, and all judgments, bonds, specialities, choses in action, and claims or debts of whatsoever description, of the territory of Wisconsin, shall enure to and vest in the state of Wisconsin and may be sued for and recovered in the same manner and to the same extent, by the state of Wisconsin, as the same could have been by the territory of Wisconsin. All criminal prosecutions and penal actions, which may have arisen, or which may arise before the change from a territorial to a state government, and which shall then be pending, shall be prosecuted to judgment and execution in the name of the state. All offences committed against the laws of the territory of Wisconsin, before the change from a territorial to a state government, and which shall not be prosecuted before such change, may be prosecuted in the name and by the authority of the state of Wisconsin, with like effect as though such change had not taken place; and all penalties incurred shall remain the same as if this constitution had not been adopted. All actions at law and suits in equity, which may be pending in any of the courts of the territory of Wiscon-in, at the time of the change from a territorial to a state government, may be continued and transferred to any court of the state which shall have jurisdiction of the subject matter thereof.

SEC. 5 All officers, civil and military, now holding their offices under the authority of the United States, or of the territory of Wisconsin, shall continue to hold and exercise their respective offices until they shall be superseded by the authority of the state.

SEC. 6. The first session of the legislature of the state of Wisconsin shall commence on the first Monday in June next, and shall be held at the village of Madison, which shall be and remain the seat of government until otherwise provided by law.

SEC. 7. All county, precinct and township officers, shall continue to hold their respective offices, unless removed by the competent authority, until the legislature shall in conformity with the provisions of this constitution, provide for the holding of elections to fill such offices respectively.

SEC. 8. The president of this convention shall immediately after its adjournment, cause a fair copy of this constitution, together with a copy of the act of the legislature of this territory, entitled "an act in relation to the formation of a state government in Wisconsin, and to change the time for holding the annual session of the legislature," approved October 26th, 1847, providing for the calling of this convention: and also a copy of so much of the last census of this territory as exhibits the number of its inhabitants, to be forwarded to the President of the United States, to be laid before the congress of the United States at its present session.

SEC. 9. This constitution shall be submitted at an election to be held on the second Monday in March next, for ratification or rejection, to all white male persons of the age of twenty-one years, or upwards, who shall then be residents of this territory, and citizens of the United States, or shall have declared their intention to become such in conformity with the laws of congress on the subject of naturalization; and all persons having such qualifications shall be entitled to vote for or against the adoption of this constitution, and for all officers first elected under it. And if the constitution be ratified by the said electors, it shall become the constitution of the state of Wisconsin. On such of the ballots as are for the constitution, shall be written or printed the word "yes;" and on such as are against the constitution, the word "no." The election shall be conducted in the manner now prescribed by law, and the returns made by the clerks of the board of supervisors or county commissioners (as the case may be) to the governor of the territory, at any time before the tenth day of April next. And in the event of the ratification of this constitution, by a majority of all the votes given, it shall be the duty of the governor of this territory to make proclamation of the same, and to transmit a digest of the returns to the senate and assembly of the state, on the first day of their session. An election shall be held for governor and lieutenant-governor, treasurer, attorney-general, members of the state legislature, and members of congress, on the second Monday of May next, and no other or further notice of such election shall be required.

SEC. 10. Two members of congress shall also be elected on the second Monday of May next; and until otherwise provided by law, the counties of Milwaukee, Waukesha, Jefferson, Racine, Walworth, Rock and Green, shall constitute the first congressional district, and elect one member; and the counties of Washington, Sheboygan, Manitowoc, Calumet, Brown, Winnebago, Fond du Lac, Marquette, Sauk, Portage, Columbia, Dodge, Dane, Iowa, La Fayette, Grant, Richland, Crawford, Chippewa, St. Croix and La Pointe, shall constitute the second congressional district, and shall elect one member.

SEC. 11. The several elections provided for in this article, shall be conducted according to the existing laws of the territory: Provided, That no elector shall be entitled to vote, except in the town, ward, or precinct where he resides. The returns of election for senators and members of assembly, shall be transmitted to the clerk of the board of supervisors, or county commissioners, as the case may be, and the votes shall be canvassed, and certificates of election issued, as now provided by law. In the first senatorial district, the returns of the election for senator shall be made to the proper officer in the county of Brown; in the second senatorial district, to the proper officer in the county of Columbia; in the third senatorial district, to the proper officer in the county of Crawford; in the fourth senatorial district, to the proper officer in the county of Fond du Lac; and in the fifth senatorial district, to the proper officer in the county of Iowa. The returns of election for state officers and members of congress, shall be certified and transmitted to the speaker of the assembly at the seat of government, in the same manner as the votes for delegates to congress are required to be certified and returned by the laws of the territory of Wisconsin, to the secretary of said territory, and in such time that they may be received on the first monday in June next; and as soon as the legislature shall be organized, the speaker of the assembly and the president of the senate shall, in the presence of both houses examine the returns, and declare who are duly elected to fill the several offices hereinbefore mentioned, and to give to each of the persons elected, a certificate of his election.

SEC. 12. Until there shall be a new apportionment, the senators and members of the assembly shall be apportioned among the several districts, as hereinafter mentioned, and each district shall be entitled to elect one senator or member of the assembly, as the case may be.

The counties of Brown, Calumet, Manitowoc and Sheboygan, shall constitute the first senate district.

The counties of Columbia, Marquette, Portage and Sauk, shall constitute the second senate district.

The counties of Crawford, Chippewa, St. Croix, and La Pointe, shall constitute the third senate district.

The counties of Fond du Lac and Winnebago, shall constitute the fourth senate district.

The counties of Iowa and Richland, shall constitute the fifth senate district.

The county of Grant shall constitute the sixth senate district.

The county of La Fayette shall constitute the seventh senate district.

The county of Green shall constitute the eighth senate district.

The county of Dane shall constitute the ninth senate district.

The county of Dodge shall constitute the tenth senate district.

The county of Washington shall constitute the eleventh senate district.

The county of Jefferson shall constitute the twelfth senate district.

The county of Waukesha shall constitute the thirteenth senate district.

The county of Walworth shall constitute the fourteenth senate district.

The county of Rock shall constitute the fifteenth senate district.

The towns of Southport, Pike, Pleasant Prairie, Paris, Bristol, Brighton, Salem and Wheatland, in the county of Racine, shall constitute the sixteenth senate district.

The towns of Racine, Caledonia, Mount Pleasant, Raymond, Norway, Rochester, Yorkville and Burlington, in the county of Racine, shall constitute the seventeenth senate district.

The third, fourth, and fifth wards of the city of Milwaukee, and the towns of Lake, Oak Creek, Franklin, and Greenfield, in the county of Milwaukee, shall constitute the eighteenth senate district.

The first and second wards of the city of Milwaukee, and the towns of Milwaukee, Wauwatosa, and Granville, in the county of Milwaukee, shall constitute the nineteenth senate district.

The county of Brown shall constitute an assembly district.

The county of Calumet shall constitute an assembly district.

The county of Manitowoc shall constitute an assembly district.

The county of Columbia shall constitute an assembly district.

The counties of Crawford and Chippewa shall constitute an assembly district.

The counties of St. Croix and La Pointe shall constitute an assembly district.

The towns of Windsor, Sun Prairie and Cottage Grove, in the county of Dane, shall constitute an assembly district.

The towns of Madison, Cross Plains, Clarkson, Springfield, Verona, Montrose, Oregon and Greenfield, in the county of Dane, shall constitute an assembly district.

The towns of Rome, Dunkirk, Christiana, Albion and Rutland, in the county of Dane, shall constitute an assembly district.

The towns of Burnett, Chester, Le Roy and Williamstown, in the county of Dodge, shall constitute an assembly district.

The towns of Fairfield, Hubbard and Rubicon, in the county of Dodge, shall constitute an assembly district.

The towns of Hustisford, Ashippun, Lebanon and Emmett, in the county of Dodge, shall constitute an assembly district.

The towns of Elba, Lowell, Portland and Clyman, in the county of Dodge, shall constitute an assembly district.

The towns of Calamus, Beaver Dam, Fox Lake and Trenton, in the county of Dodge, shall constitute an assembly district.

The towns of Calumet, Forest, Auburn, Byron, Taychedah and Fond du Lac, in the county of Fond du Lac, shall constitute an assembly district.

The towns of Alto, Metoman, Ceresco, Rosendale, Waupun, Oakfield and Seven Mile Creek, in the county of Fond du Lac, shall constitute an assembly district.

The precincts of Hazel Green, Fairplay, Smeltzer's Grove and Jamestown, in the county of Grant, shall constitute an assembly district.

The precincts of Platteville, Head of Platte, Centerville, Muscoday and Fennimore, in the county of Grant, shall constitute an assembly district.

The precincts of Pleasant Valley, Potosi, Waterloo, Hurricane and New Lisbon, in the county of Grant, shall constitute an assembly district.

The precincts of Beetown, Patch Grove, Cassville, Millville and Lancaster, in the county of Grant, shall constitute an assembly district.

The county of Green shall constitute an assembly district.

The precincts of Dallas, Peddlar's Creek, Mineral Point and Yellow Stone, in the county of Iowa, shall constitute an assembly district.

The precincts of Franklin, Dodgeville, Porter's Grove, Arena and Percussion, in the county of Iowa, and the county of Richland, shall constitute an assembly district.

The towns of Watertown, Aztalan and Waterloo, in the county of Jefferson, shall constitute an assembly district.

The towns of Ixonia, Concord, Sullivan, Hebron, Cold Spring

and Palmyra, in the county of Jefferson, shall constitute an assembly district.

The towns of Lake Mills, Oakland, Koskonong, Farmington and Jefferson, in the county of Jefferson, shall constitute an assembly district.

The precincts of Benton, Elk Grove, Belmont, Willow Springs, Prairie and that part of Shullsburgh precinct north of town one, in the county of La Fayette, shall constitute an assembly district.

The precincts of Wiota, Wayne, Gratiot, White Oak Springs, Fever River, and that part of Shullsburgh precinct south of town two, in the county of La Fayette, shall constitute an assembly district.

The county of Marquette shall constitute an assembly district.

The first ward of the city of Milwaukee shall constitute an assembly district.

The second ward of the city of Milwaukee shall constitute an assembly district.

The third ward of the city of Milwaukee shall constitute an assembly district.

The fourth and fifth wards of the city of Milwaukee shall constitute an assembly district.

The towns of Franklin and Oak Creek, in the county of Milwaukee, shall constitute an assembly district.

The towns of Greenfield and Lake, in the county of Milwaukee, shall constitute an assembly district.

The towns of Granville, Wauwatosa and Milwaukee, in the county of Milwaukee, shall constitute an assembly district.

The county of Portage shall constitute an assembly district.

The town of Racine, in the county of Racine, shall constitute an assembly district.

The towns of Norway, Raymond, Caledonia and Mount Pleasant, in the county of Racine, shall constitute an assembly district.

The towns of Rochester, Burlington and Yorkville, in the county of Racine, shall constitute an assembly district.

The towns of Southport, Pike and Pleasant Prairie, in the county of Racine, shall constitute an assembly district.

The towns of Paris, Bristol, Brighton, Salem and Wheatland, in the county of Racine, shall constitute an assembly district.

The towns of Janesville and Bradford, in the county of Rock, shall constitute an assembly district.

The towns of Beloit, Turtle and Clinton, in the county of Rock, shall constitute an assembly district.

The towns of Magnolia, Union, Porter and Fulton, in the county of Rock, shall constitute an assembly district.

The towns of Milton, Lima and Johnstown, in the county of Rock, shall constitute an assembly district.

The towns of Newark, Rock, Avon, Spring Valley and Center, in the county of Rock, shall constitute an assembly district: Provided, that if the legislature shall divide the town of Center, they may attach such part of it to the district lying next north, as they may deem expedient.

The county of Sauk shall constitute an assembly district.

Precincts numbered one, three and seven, in the county of Sheboygan, shall constitute an assembly district.

Precincts numbered two, four, five and six, in the county of Sheboygan, shall constitute an assembly district.

The towns of Troy, East Troy and Spring Prairie, in the county of Walworth, shall constitute an assembly district.

The towns of Whitewater, Richmond and La Grange, in the county of Walworth, shall constitute an assembly district.

The towns of Geneva, Hudson, and Bloomfield, in the county of Walworth, shall constitute an assembly district.

The towns of Darien, Sharon, Walworth and Linn, in the county of Walworth, shall constitute an assembly district.

The towns of Delavan, Sugar Creek, La Fayette and Elkhorn, in the county of Walworth, shall constitute an assembly district.

The towns of Lisbon, Menomonee and Brookfield, in the county of Waukesha, shall constitute an assembly district.

6

The towns of Warren, Oconomowoc, Summit and Ottawa, in the county of Waukesha, shall constitute an assembly district.

The towns of Delafield, Genesee and Pewaukee, in the county of Waukesha, shall constitute an assembly district.

The towns of Waukesha and New Berlin, in the county of Waukesha, shall constitute an assembly district.

The towns of Eagle, Mukwonago, Vernon and Muskego, in the county of Waukesha, shall constitute an assembly district.

The towns of Port Washington, Fredonia and Clarence, in the county of Washington, shall constitute an assembly district.

The towns of Grafton and Jackson, in the county of Washington, shall constitute an assembly district.

The towns of Mequon and Germantown, in the county of Washington, shall constitute an assembly district.

The towns of Polk, Richfield and Erin, in the county of Washington, shall constitute an assembly district.

The towns of Hartford, Addison, West Bend and North Bend, in the county of Washington, shall constitute an assembly district.

The county of Winnebago shall constitute an assembly district.

The foregoing districts are subject, however, so far to be altered that when any new town shall be organized, it may be added to either of the adjoining assembly districts.

SEC. 13. Such parts of the common law as are now in force in the territory of Wisconsin, not inconsistent with this constitution, shall be and continue part of the law of this state until altered or suspended by the legislature.

SEC. 14. The senators first elected in the even numbered senate districts, the governor, lieutenant governor, and other state officers, first elected under this constitution, shall enter upon the duties of their respective offices on the first Monday of June next, and shall continue in office for one year from the first Monday of January next. The senators first elected in the odd numbered senate districts, and the members of the assembly first elected, shall enter upon their duties respectively on the first Monday of June next, and shall continue in office until the first Monday in January next.

SEC. 15. The oath of office may be administered by any judge or justice of the peace, until the legislature shall otherwise direct.

RESOLUTIONS.

RESOLVED—That the congress of the United States be, and is hereby requested, upon the application of Wisconsin for admission into the Union, so to alter the provisions of an act of congress entitled "an act to grant a quantity of land to the territory of Wisconsin, for the purpose of aiding in opening a canal to connect the waters of Lake Michigan with those of Rock River," approved June eighteenth, eighteen hundred and thirty-eight; and so to alter the terms and conditions of the grant made therein, that the odd numbered sections thereby granted and remaining unsold, may be held and disposed of by the State of Wisconsin, as part of the five hundred thousand acres of land to which said state is entitled by the provisions of an act of congress, entitled "an act to appropriate the proceeds of the sales of the public lands, and to grant pre-emption rights," approved the fourth day of September, eighteen hundred and forty-one ; and further, that the even numbered sections reserved by congress may be offered for sale by the United States for the same minimum price, and subject to the same rights of pre-emption as other public lands of the United States.

RESOLVED—That congress be further requested to pass an act whereby the excess price over and above one dollar and twenty-five cents per acre, which may have been paid by the purchasers of said even numbered sections which shall have been sold by the United States, be refunded to the present owners thereof, or they be allowed to enter any of the public lands of the United States, to an amount equal in value to the excess so paid.

RESOLVED—That in case the odd numbered sections shall be ceded to the state as aforesaid, the same shall be sold by the state in the same manner as other school lands: Provided, That the same rights of pre-emption as are now granted by the laws of the United States shall be secured to persons who may be actually settled upon such lands at the time of the adoption of this constitution: And provided further, That the excess price over and above one dollar and twenty-five cents per acre, absolutely or conditionally contracted to be paid by the purchasers of any part of said sections which shall have been sold by the territory of Wisconsin, shall be remitted to such purchasers, their representatives, or assigns.

RESOLVED—That congress be requested, upon the application of Wisconsin for admission into the Union, to pass an act whereby the grant of five hundred thousand acres of land, to which the state of Wisconsin is entitled by the provisions of an act of congress entitled "an act to appropriate the proceeds of the sales of the public lands, and to grant pre-emption rights," approved the fourth day of September, eighteen hundred and forty-one, and also the five per centum of the nett proceeds of the public lands lying within the state, to which it shall become entitled on its admission into the Union, by the provisions of an act of congress, entitled "an act to enable the people of Wisconsin territory to form a constitution and state government, and for the admission of such state into the Union," approved the 6th day of August, eighteen hundred and forty-six, shall be granted to the state of Wisconsin for the use of schools, instead of the purposes mentioned in said acts of congress respectively.

RESOLVED—That the congress of the United States be, and hereby is requested, upon the admission of this state into the Union, so to alter the provisions of the act of congress, entitled "an act to grant a certain quantity of land to aid in the improvement of the Fox and Wisconsin rivers, and to connect the same by a canal in the territory of Wisconsin," that the price of the lands reserved to the United States, shall be reduced to the minimum price of the public lands.

RESOLVED—That the legislature of this state shall make provision by law for the sale of the lands granted to the state in aid of said improvements, subject to the same rights of pre-emption to the settlers thereon, as are now allowed by law to settlers on the public lands.

RESOLVED—That the foregoing resolutions be appended to and signed with the constitution of Wisconsin, and submitted therewith to the people of this territory, and to the congress of the United States.

———

We, the undersigned, members of the convention to form a constitution for the state of Wisconsin, to be submitted to the people thereof for their ratification or rejection, do hereby certify that the foregoing is the constitution adopted by the convention.

In testimony whereof, we have hereunto set our hands, at Madison, the first day of February, A. D. eighteen hundred and forty-eight.

MORGAN L. MARTIN,
President of the Convention, and Delegate
from Brown County.

THOMAS McHUGH, Secretary.

Calumet.
G. W. Featherstonhaugh.

Columbia.
James T. Lewis.

Crawford.
Daniel G. Fenton.

Dane.
William H. Fox.
Charles M. Nichols.
William A. Wheeler.

Dodge.
Stoddard Judd.
Charles H. Larrabee.
Samuel W. Lyman.

Fond du Lac.
Samuel W. Beall.
Warren Chase.

Grant.
Orasmus Cole.
George W. Lakin.
Alexander D. Ramsey.
William Richardson.
John H. Rountree.

Green.
James Biggs.

Iowa.
Charles Bishop.
Stephen Hollenbeck.
Joseph Ward.

Jefferson.
Jonas Folts.
Milo Jones.
Theodore Prentiss.
Abraham Vanderpool.

La Fayette.
Charles Dunn.
John O'Connor.
Allen Warden.

Milwaukee.
John L. Doran.
Garrett M. Fitzgerald.
Albert Fowler.
Byron Kilbourn.
Rufus King.
Charles H. Larkin.
Morritz Schoeffler.

Portage.
William H. Kennedy.

Racine.
Albert G. Cole.
Stephen A. Davenport.
Andrew B. Jackson.
Frederick S. Lovell.
Samuel R. McClellan.
James D. Reymert.
Horace T. Sanders.
Theodore Secor.

Rock.
Almerin M. Carter.
Joseph Colley.
Paul Crandall.
Ezra A. Foote.
Louis P. Harvey.
Edward V. Whiton.

Sheboygan.
Silas Steadman.

Walworth.
Experience Estabrook.
George Gale.
James Harrington.
Augustus C. Kinne.
Hollis Latham.
Ezra A. Mulford.

Washington.
James Fagan.
Patrick Pentony.
Harvey G. Turner.

Waukesha.
Squire S. Case.
Alfred L. Castleman.
Peter D. Gifford.
Eleazer Root.
George Scagel.

Winnebago.
Harrison Reed.

CENSUS OF COUNTIES IN 1836, 1840, & 1850.

LIST OF TOWNS BY COUNTIES, WITH POPULATION IN 1836, AND EVERY SUBSEQUENT CENSUS, WHETHER BY STATE OR GENERAL GOVERNMENT.

ADAMS COUNTY.

Population of the County in 1850 . . . 187

BAD AX COUNTY.

Town of Bad Ax.

BROWN COUNTY.

Town of Green Bay.   Wrightstown.
          Depere.   Lawrence.
          Howard.   Pittsfield.

Population of the County in 1836 . . 2,776
do.   do.   in 1840 . . 2,107
do.   do.   in 1850 . . 6,222

CALUMET COUNTY.

Town of Stockbridge.   Charlestown.
          Manchester.   New Holstein.

Population of the County in 1840 . . 275
do.   do.   in 1850 . . 1,745

CHIPPEWA COUNTY.

Population of the County in 1850 . . 615

CRAWFORD COUNTY.

Town of Prairie du Chien.

Population of the County in 1886 . . 850
do.   do.   in 1840 . . 1,502
do.   do.   in 1850 . . 2,399

COLUMBIA COUNTY.

Town of Columbus.	Springville.
Hampden.	Wyocena.
Leeds.	Caledonia.
Lodi.	Portage City.
West Point.	Port Hope.
Dekora.	Marcellon.
Lowville.	Scott.
Otsego.	Randolph.
Fountain Prairie.	Lewiston.
Courtland.	

Population of the County in 1850 . . 9,565

DANE COUNTY.

Town of Madison.	Sun Prairie.
Albion.	Verona.
Blooming Grove.	Windsor.
Bristol.	York.
Burke.	Berry.
Christiana.	Cross Plains.
Cottage Grove.	Black Earth.
Dunkirk.	Dane.
Dunn.	Springfield.
Deerfield.	Roxbury.
Medina.	Vienna.
Middleton.	Westport.
Montrose.	Blue Mounds.

DANE COUNTY continued.

Town of Oregon.   Deerfield.
   Pleasant Springs. Primrose.
   Rutland.   · Spring Dale.

Population of the County in 1840 . . 314
  do.   do.   in 1850 . . 16,654

DODGE COUNTY.

Town of Hubbard. Theresa.
   Rubicon.   Lowell.
   Herman.   Portland.
   Westford.   Calamus.
   Emmett.   Asshippin.
   Lebanon.   Oak Grove.
   Elba.   Beaver Dam.
   Trenton.   Leroy.
   Chester.   Lomira.
   Williamstown. Clyman.
   Shields.   Fox Lake.
   Hustisford. Burnett.

Population of the County in 1840 . . 67
  do.   do.   in 1850 . . 14,502

DOOR COUNTY.

FOND DU LAC COUNTY.

City of Fond du Lac. Taycheedah.
Town of Fond du Lac. Oakfield.
   Friendship. Waupun.
   Byron.   Alto.
   Eden.   Metomen.
   Ashford.   Spring Vale.
   Auburn.   Lamartine.

7

FOND DU LAC COUNTY continued.

Osceola.
Forest.
Empire.
Calumet.

Eldorado.
Rosendale.
Ceresco.

Population of the County in 1840 . . 139
do.　　do.　　in 1850 . . 14,512

GRANT COUNTY.

Town of Beetown.
Smelser.
Potosi.
Patch Grove.
Lancaster.
Cassville.
Clifton.
Wingville.
Hazel Green.
Jamestown.

Muscoda.
Platteville.
Highland.
Lima.
Waterloo.
Harrison.
Paris.
Fennamore.
Liberty.
Ellenborough.

Population of the County in 1840 . . 3,926
do.　　do.　　in 1850 . . 16,196

GREEN COUNTY.

Town of Albany.
Adams.
Brooklyn.
Cadiz.
Clarno.
Decatur.
Exeter.
Jordon.

Jefferson.
Mount Pleasant.
Monroe.
Spring Grove.
New Glarus.
Washington.
Sylvester.
York.

Population of the County in 1840 . . 933
do.　　do.　　in 1850 . . 8,583

IOWA COUNTY.

Town of Arena.　　　　　　Mineral Point.
　　　Clyde.　　　　　　　' Pulaski.
　　　Dodgeville.　　　　　Ridgeway.
　　　Highland.　　　　　　Waldwic.
　　　Linden.　　　　　　　Wyoming.
　　　Mifflin.

Population of the County in 1840　.　.　8,978
　　do.　　do.　　in 1850　.　.　9,576

JEFFERSON COUNTY.

Town of Aztalan.　　　　　Lake Mills.
　　　Concord.　　　　　　Milford.
　　　Coldspring.　　　　　Oakland.
　　　Farmington.　　　　　Palmyra.
　　　Hebron.　　　　　　Sullivan.
　　　Ixonia.　　　　　　Watertown.
　　　Jefferson.　　　　　Waterloo.
　　　Koshkonong.

Population of the County in 1840　.　.　914
　　do.　　do.　　in 1850　.　.　15,339

KENOSHA COUNTY.

Town of Bristol.　　　　　Somers.
　　　Pleasant Prairie.　　Brighton.
　　　Salem.　　　　　　Wheatland.
　　　Southport.　　　　Kenosha.
　　　Paris.

Population of the County in 1850　.　.　10,730

KEWAUNEE COUNTY.

Town of Kewaunee.

LA CROSS COUNTY.

Town of Albion.　　　　　Neshonoe.
　　　Pine Valley.　　　　Pierce.
　　　Monteville.　　　　Leon.

LAFAYETTE COUNTY:

Town of Fayette.	White Oak Springs.
Wiota.	Gratiot.
Elk Grove.	Centre.
Wayne.	Argyle.
New Diggings.	Willow Springs.
Shullsburgh.	Monticello.
Kendall.	Belmont.
Benton.	

Population of the County in 1850 . . 11,556

LA POINTE COUNTY.

Town of La Pointe.

Population of the County in 1850 . . . 595

MANITOWOC COUNTY.

Town of Manitowoc.	Newson.
Two Rivers.	Maple Grove.
Meeme.	Centreville.
Kossuth.	Edson.
Manitowoc Rapids.	

Population of the County in 1840 . . 235
    do.   do.   in 1850 . . 3,712

MARATHON COUNTY.

Population of the County in 1850 . . . 466

MARQUETTE COUNTY.

Town of Berlin.	Buffalo.
Brooklin.	Packwaukee.
Mackford.	Montello.
Green Lake.	Moundville.
Dayton.	Neshkora.

MARQUETTE COUNTY continued.

Town of Hardin.	Shields.
Kingston.	Crystal Lake.
Princeton.	Oxford.
Marquette.	Westfield.

Population of the County in 1840 . . 18
do. do. in 1850 . . 8,642

MILWAUKEE COUNTY.

City of Milwaukee.	Lake.
Town of Milwaukee.	Granville.
Wauwatosa.	Franklin.
Greenfield.	Oak Creek.

Population of the County in 1836 . . 2,893
do. do. in 1840 . . 5,605
do. do. in 1850 . . 31,116

OUTAGAMIE COUNTY.

Town of Grand Chute.	Hontonia.
Kaukauna.	Freedom.
Ellington.	Lansing.
Greenville.	Medina.

OCONTO COUNTY.

PORTAGE COUNTY.

| Town of Plover. | Grand Rapids. |
| Stevens' Point. | |

Population of the County in 1840 . . 1,623
do. do. in 1850 . . 1,267

RACINE COUNTY.

City of Racine.	Yorkville.
Town of Racine.	Norway.
Mount Pleasant.	Dover.
Caledonia.	Burlington.
Raymond.	Rochester.

Population of the County in 1840 . . **3,475**
    do.   do.   in 1850 . . **14,971**

RICHLAND COUNTY.

Town of Richwood.	Rockbridge.
Richmond.	Richland.
Buena Vista.	

Population of the County in 1850 . . . **963**

ROCK COUNTY.

Town of Avon.	Lima.
Beloit.	Magnolia.
Bradford.	Milton.
Centre.	Newark.
Clinton.	Plymouth.
Fulton.	Porter.
Harmony.	Rock.
Janesville.	Spring Valley.
Johnstown.	Turtle.
La Prairie.	Union.

Population of the County in 1840 . . **1,701**
    do.   do.   in 1850 . . **20,717**

SAINT CROIX COUNTY.

Town of Prescott.	Falls of St. Croix.
Kinnikennic.	Hudson.
Rush River.	Le Roys.

Population of the County in 1840 . . . **809**
    do.   do.   in 1850 . . . **624**

SAUK COUNTY.

Town of Brooklyn.	Lemonneir.
Dellona.	Marston.
Flora.	New Buffalo.
Freedom.	Prairie du Sac.
Honey Creek.	Reedsburgh.
Kingston.	Spring Green.
Kildare.	

Population of the County in 1840 . . 102
    do.   do.   in 1850 . . 4,372

SHEBOYGAN COUNTY.

Town of Sheboygan.	Plymouth.
Lima.	Linden.
Wilson.	Abbott.
Hermann.	Sheboygan Falls.
Scott.	Holland.
Mitchell.	Rhimer.
Greenbush.	

Population of the County in 1840 . . 133
    do.   do.   in 1850 . . 8,386

WALWORTH COUNTY.

Town of Sharon.	Geneva.
Darien.	Lafayette.
Richmond.	Troy.
Whitewater.	East Troy.
Lagrange.	Spring Prairie.
Sugar Creek.	Hudson.
Delavan.	Bloomfield.
Walworth.	Elkhorn.
Linn.	

Population of the County in 1840 . . 2,611
    do.   do.   in 1850 . . 17,866

WASHINGTON COUNTY.

Town of Port Washington.	West Bend.
Grafton.	Polk.
Cedarburgh.	Richfield.
Mequon.	Hartford.
Germantown.	Addison.
Jackson.	Trenton.
Saukville.	Farmington.
Belgium.	Kewaskum.
Fredonia.	Erin.
Newark.	Wayne.

Population of the County in 1840 . . 343
do. do. in 1850 . . 19,476

WAUKESHA COUNTY.

Town of Merton.	Muskego.
Menomonee.	Waukesha.
Summet.	Eagle.
Lisbon.	Ottawa.
Mukwonago.	Pewaukee.
Oconomowoc.	Brookfield.
Genesee.	New Berlin.
Vernon.	Delafield.

Population of the County in 1850 . . 19,324

WAUSHARA COUNTY.

Town of Mount Morris.	Ontario.
Pine River.	Marion.
Oasis.	Wautoma.

WAUPACA COUNTY.

Town of Mukwa.	Weyawega.
Lind.	Centreville.
Waupaca.	Dayton.

WINNEBAGO COUNTY.

Town of Algoma.   Rushford.
        Black Wolf.   Utica.
        Omro.   Vinland.
        Clayton.   Oshkosh.
        Neenah.   Winneconne.
        Nepeuskum.   Winchester.
        Nekama.

Population of the County in 1840 . .   135
    do.   do.   in 1850 . . 19,179

———

Total Population of Wisconsin in 1850 . . . 305,528
    do.   do.   in 1840 . . . 30,945
    do.   do.   in 1836 . . .   6,449

POST OFFICES IN WISCONSIN.

LIST OF POST OFFICES, WITH NAME OF COUNTY, AND WHERE SITUATED.

BROWN COUNTY.

Bridgeport.	Green Bay.	Little Chute.
Cooperstown.	Greenville.	Mukwa.
Depere, (c. h.)	Hortonville.	Oneida.
Fremont.	Lansing.	

CALUMET COUNTY.

Charlestown.	New Holstein.	Pigeon Grove.
Dundas.	Pequot.	Stockbridge.

CHIPPEWA COUNTY.

Clearwater.	Nelson's Landing.
Middle Mills.	Ogalla.

COLUMBIA COUNTY.

Bellefontaine.	Hampden.	Pigeon Grove.
Centreville.	Lodi.	Portage City.
Columbus.	Lowerville.	Port Hope.
Dekorra.	Marcellon.	Poynett.
Fall River.	Oshaukuta.	Randolph.
Fort Winnebago.	Otsego.	Rocky Run.
Grand Marsh.	Pardeeville.	Wyocena.

CRAWFORD COUNTY.

Bad Axe.
Black River Falls.
Coon Prairie.
Elk.
La Crosse.
Mount Sterling.
Prairie du Chien.
Springville.
Warner's Landing.

DANE COUNTY.

Albion.
Ancient.
Ashton.
Baas Lake.
Berry.
Black Earth.
Blue Mound.
Cambridge.
Christiana.
Cottage Grove.
Cross Plains.
Dane.
Deerfield.
Door Creek.
Dunkirk.
Eolia.
Fitchburg.
Grand Spring.
Hanchetville.
Lake View.
Madison.
Middleton.
Oregon.
Pheasant Branch.
Pierceville.
Pine Bluff.
Primrose.
Rutland.
Springdale.
Stoner's Prairie.
Stoughton.
Sun Prairie.
Turkey Grove.
Utica.
Verona.
Windsor.
York.

DODGE COUNTY.

Asshippun.
Beaver Dam.
Burnett.
Burnett Corner.
Chester.
Clyman.
Elba.
Emmett.
Farmersville.
Hermann.
Horicon.
Hustisford.
Iron Ridge.
Juneau.
Leroy.
Lomira.
Lowell.
Mayville.
Neosha.
Oak Grove.
Theresa.
Trenton Corners.
Waushara.

FOND DU LAC COUNTY.

Alcove.
Alto.
Auburn.
Avoca.
Badger.
Bothelle.
Byron.
Calumet Village.
Ceresco.

FOND DU LAC COUNTY continued.

Dotyville.
Eden.
El Dorado.
Fairwater.
Fond du Lac.
Friendship.

Lamartine.
Metomen.
Oakfield.
Owascus.
Rock River.
Rosendale.

Rush Lake.
Springvale.
Taycheedah.
Waupun.
West Rosendale.

GRANT COUNTY.

Beetown.
Cassville.
Dickeysville.
Ellenborough.
Fair Play.
Fennimore.
Hazel Green.

Hurricane Grove.
Jamestown.
Lancaster.
Millville.
Montfort.
Muscoda.
New California.

Pin Hook.
Platteville.
Potosi.
Smeltzer's Grove.
Ursine.
Wyalusing.

GREEN COUNTY.

Albany.
Attica.
Bem.
Cadiz.
Clarence.
Decatur.
Exeter.

Farmer's Grove.
Hoosick.
Hoosier Grove.
India.
Monroe.
Montezuma.
Monticello.

Mount Pleasant.
Nevada.
New Glarus.
Spring Grove.
Sylvester.
Walnut Springs.
Willet.

IOWA COUNTY.

Arena.
Blue River.
Dodgeville.
Dover.
Elk Grove.
Helena.

Highland.
Linden.
Mifflin.
Mineral Point.
Ridgeway.
Waldwick.

Wallace.
White Oak Springs.
Willow Springs.
Wyoming.

JEFFERSON COUNTY.

Aztalan.
Bark River.
ColdSpring.
Concord.
Farmington.
Fort Atkinson.
Helenville.
Hubbleton.

Lyonia.
Jefferson.
Koshkonong.
Lake Mills.
Milford.
Newton Corners.
Oak Hills.
Oakland.

Oénca.
Palmyra.
Rome.
Sullivan.
Waterloo.
Watertown.

KENOSHA COUNTY.

Brighton.
Bristol.
Kenosha.

Marion.
Paris.
Pleasant Grove.

Wheatland.
Wilmot.

LA FAYETTE COUNTY.

Argyle.
Benton.
Cottage Inn.
Fayette.

Georgetown.
Gratiot.
Hamilton.
New Diggings.

Shullsburgh.
Saint Mary's.
Wiota.

MANITOWOC COUNTY.

Collins.
Francis Creek.
Manitowoc.

Manitowoc Rapids.
Meeme.

Mishcott.
Two Rivers.

MARATHON COUNTY.

Wausau.

MARQUETTE COUNTY.

Berlin.
Blufton.
Dartford.
Grand Prairie.

Green Lake.
Greewood.
Harrisville.
Kingston.

Lake Maria.
Markesan.
Marquette.
Montello.

MARQUETTE COUNTY continued.

Moundville.
Namahkun.
Neshkoro.
Oasis.
Packwaukee.
Pine River.

Poy Sippi.
Princeton.
Rock Hill.
Roslin.
Roxo.
Sacramento.

Techora.
Warwick.
Waupaka.
Wautoma.
Westfield.
Willow Creek.

MILWAUKEE COUNTY.

Butler.
Franklin.
Good Hope.
Granville.

Greenfield.
Milwaukee.
Muskego.
New Berlin.

Oak Creek.
Root Creek.
Wauwatosa.

OUTAGAMIE COUNTY.

Ellington.

Kaukauna.

PORTAGE COUNTY.

Almond.
Buena Vista.
Eau Pleine.

Grand Rapids.
Plover.
Steven's Point.

Warsaw.

RACINE COUNTY.

Burlington.
Caldwell Prairie.
Caledonia.
Hoadly.
Ives' Grove.
Kossuth.
Liberty.

Mount Pleasant.
Norway.
Pen Yen.
Racine.
Raymond.
Rochester.
Salem.

South Bristol.
Sylvania.
Thompsonville.
Union Grove.
Waterford.
Yorkville.

RICHLAND COUNTY.

Orion.
Richland City.

Sand Prairie.
Sextonville.

ROCK COUNTY.

Avon.	Janesville.	Rock-Prairie.
Bachelors' Grove.	Johnstown.*	Rock Valley.
Beloit.	Johnstown Centre.	Shopiere.
Centre.	Leyden.	Spring Valley.
Clinton.	Lima.	Summerville.
Cooksville.	Magnolia.	Teotsa.
Emerald Grove.	Milton.	Union.
Evansville.	Newark.	Warren.
Fulton.	North Janesville.	
Inmansville.	Osborn.	

ST. CROIX COUNTY.

Brock's Crossing.	La Pointe.	Willow River.
Falls of St. Croix.	Marine Mills.	

SAUK COUNTY.

Baraboo.	Dellona.	Reedsburgh.
Bear Creek.	Freedom.	Russell's Corners.
Bluff.	Leland's Mill.	Seven-mile Creek.
Colamer.	Oneonta.	
Dalton.	Prairie du Sac.	

SHEBOYGAN COUNTY.

Cascade.	Howard's Grove.	Rathbun.
Cedar Grove.	Mentor.	Scott.
Elkhart.	Mitchell.	Sheboygan (c. h.)
Gibbville.	Onion River.	Sheboygan Falls.
Greenbush.	Plymouth.	Worth.

WALWORTH COUNTY.

Adams.	Darien.	Geneva.
Allen's Grove.	Delavan.	Geneva Bay.
Baker's Corners.	East Troy.	Genoa.
Big Foot Prairie.	Elkhorn (c. h.)	Heart Prairie.
Bloomfield.	Fairfield.	Honev Creek.

WALWORTH COUNTY continued.

Lafayette.	Sharon.	Troy Centre.
La Grange.	South Grove.	Troy Lakes.
Little Prairie.	Spring Prairie.	Utter's Corners.
Lyons.	State Line.	Vienna.
Millard.	Sugar Creek.	Walworth.
Richmond.	Troy.	Whitewater.

WASHINGTON COUNTY.

Addison.	Grafton.	Saukville.
Barton.	Hartford.	Schlesingerville.
Cedarburgh.	Kewaskum.	Toland's Prairie.
Cedar Creek.	Mequon River.	Ulao.
Cherryhill.	Meeker.	West Bend.
Fillmore.	Newburgh.	Young Hickory.
Fredonia.	Ozaukee.	

WAUKESHA COUNTY.

Big Bend.	Lisbon.	Okauchee.
Brookfield.	Mapleton.	Ottawa.
Bullion.	Marcy.	Pewaukee.
Delafield.	Menomonee Falls.	Prospect Hill.
Denoon.	Merton.	South Genesee.
Eagleville.	Monches.	Summit.
Genesee.	Monterey.	Sussex.
Golden Lake.	Mukwonago.	Vernon.
Hartland.	Muskego Centre.	Waterville.
Howard.	Oconomowoc.	Waukesha.

WINNEBAGO COUNTY.

Algoma.	Fisk's Corners.	Nepeuskum.
Appleton.	Groveland.	Oshkosh.
Black Wolf.	Koro.	Omro.
Bloomingdale.	Lind.	Vinland.
Butte des Morts.	Menasha.	Waukau.
Clanville.	Mukwa.	Welaunee.
Delhi.	Neenah.	Weyauwega.
Eureka.	Nekemi.	

LIST OF SENATE AND ASSEMBLY DISTRICTS.

AN ACT TO APPORTION AND DISTRICT ANEW THE MEMBERS OF THE SENATE AND ASSEMBLY OF THE STATE OF WISCONSIN.

The People of the State of Wisconsin, represented in Senate and Assembly, do enact as follows :

SENATE DISTRICTS.

SECTION 1. Until there shall be a new apportionment, the senators and members of the assembly shall be apportioned among the several districts of this state as is hereinafter mentioned ; and each district shall be entitled to elect one senator or member of the assembly, as the case may be.

The counties of Sheboygan, Calumet and Manitowoc shall constitute the first senate district.

The counties of Brown, Door, Outagamie, Oconto, Waupaca, Marathon and Portage, shall constitute the second senate district.

The towns of Mequon, Cedarburg, Grafton, Port Washington, Saukville, Fredonia and Belgium, in the county of Washington, shall constitute the third senate district.

The towns of Erin, Richfield, Germantown, Jackson, Polk, Hartford, Addison, West Bend, Newark, Trenton, Farmington, Kewaskum and Wayne, in the county of Washington, shall constitute the fourth senate district.

9

The first and second wards of the city of Milwaukee, and towns of Wauwatosa, Milwaukee and Granville, in the county of Milwaukee, shall constitute the fifth senate district.

The third, fourth and fifth wards in the city of Milwaukee, and the towns of Greenfield, Lake, Oak Creek and Franklin, in the county of Milwaukee, shall constitute the sixth senate district.

The county of Racine shall constitute the seventh senate district.

The county of Kenosha shall constitute the eighth senate district.

The towns of Oconomowoc, Merton, Lisbon, Menomonee, Summit, Delafield, Pewaukee and Brookfield, in the county of Waukesha, shall constitute the ninth senate district.

The towns of Ottawa, Genesee, Waukesha, New Berlin, Muskego, Vernon, Mukwanago and Eagle, in the county of Waukesha, shall constitute the tenth senate district.

The county of Dane shall constitute the eleventh senate district.

The county of Walworth shall constitute the twelfth senate district.

The county of La Fayette shall constitute the thirteenth senate district.

The county of Jefferson shall constitute the fourteenth senate district.

The counties of Iowa and Richland shall constitute the fifteenth senate district.

The county of Grant shall constitute the sixteenth senate district.

The towns of Janesville, Rock, Fulton, Porter, Centre, Plymouth, Newark, Avon, Spring Valley, Magnolia and Union, in the county of Rock, shall constitute the seventeenth senate district.

The towns of Beloit, Turtle, Clinton, Bradford, La Prairie, Harmony, Johnstown, Lima and Milton, in the county of Rock, shall constitute the eighteenth senate district.

The counties of Crawford, La Crosse, Bad Ax, St. Croix, Chippewa and La Pointe, shall constitute the nineteenth senate district.

The county of Fond du Lac shall constitute the twentieth senate district.

The county of Winnebago shall constitute the twenty-first senate district.

The county of Dodge shall constitute the twenty-second senate district.

The counties of Marquette, Waushara, Sauk and Adams shall constitute the twenty-third senate district.

The county of Green shall constitute the twenty-fourth senate district.

The county of Columbia shall constitute the twenty-fifth senate district.

ASSEMBLY DISTRICTS.

The county of Manitowoc shall constitute an assembly district.

The county of Calumet shall constitute an assembly district.

Precincts numbered one, three and seven, in the county of Sheboygan, shall constitute an assembly district.

Precincts numbered two, four, five and six, in the county of Sheboygan, shall constitute an assembly district.

The counties of Brown, Kewaunee and Door shall constitute an assembly district.

The counties of Outagamie, Waupacca and Oconto, shall constitute an assembly district.

The counties of Portage and Marathon shall constitute an assembly district.

The towns of Belgium, Fredonia, Saukville and Port Washington, in the county of Washington, shall constitute an assembly district.

The towns of Cedarburg, Grafton and Mequon, in the county of Washington, shall constitute an assembly district.

The towns of Erin, Richfield, Polk, Jackson and Germantown, in the county of Washington, shall constitute an assembly district.

The towns of Hartford, Addison, Wayne, Kewaskum, Newark, West Bend, Trenton and Farmington, in the county of Washington, shall constitute an assembly district.

The first ward in the city of Milwaukee shall constitute an assembly district.

The second ward in the city of Milwaukee shall constitute an assembly district.

The third ward in the city of Milwaukee shall constitute an assembly district.

The fourth ward in the city of Milwaukee shall constitute an assembly district.

The fifth ward in the city of Milwaukee shall constitute an assembly district.

The towns of Franklin and Oak Creek, in the county of Milwaukee, shall constitute an assembly district.

The towns of Greenfield and Lake, in the county of Milwaukee, shall constitute an assembly district.

The town of Wauwatosa, in the county of Milwaukee, shall constitute an assembly district.

The towns of Milwaukee and Granville, [in the county of Milwaukee,] shall constitute an assembly district.

The city of Racine shall constitute an assembly district.

The towns of Racine, Mount Pleasant and Caledonia, in the county of Racine, shall constitute an assembly district.

The towns of Yorkville, Dover, Raymond and Norway, in the county of Racine, shall constitute an assembly district.

The towns of Burlington and Rochester, in the county of Racine, shall constitute an assembly district.

The city of Kenosha, and the towns of Southport, Somers and Pleasant Prairie, in the county of Kenosha, shall constitute an assembly district.

The towns of Paris, Bristol, Brighton, Salem and Wheatland, in the county of Kenosha, shall constitute an assembly district.

The towns of Merton, Delafield, Summit and Oconomowoc, in the county of Waukesha, shall constitute an assembly district.

The towns of Pewaukee, Lisbon, Menomonee and Brookfield, in the county of Waukesha, shall constitute an asssembly district.

The towns of Ottawa, Genesee. Mukwonago and Eagle, in the county of Waukesha, shall constitute an assembly district.

The towns of Waukesha, Vernon, Muskego and New Berlin, in the county of Waukesha, shall constitute an assembly district.

The towns of Dunkirk, Christiana, Pleasant Springs and Albion, in the county of Dane, shall constitute an assembly district.

The towns of Cottage Grove, Deerfield, Sun Prairie, Medina, York and Bristol, in the county of Dane, shall constitute an assembly district.

The towns of Verona, Montrose, Oregon, Greenfield, Dunn and Rutland, in the county of Dane, shall constitute an assembly district.

The towns of Perry, Primrose, Blue Mounds, Springdale, Cross Plains, Middleton, Springfield, Berry, Black Earth, Roxbury and Dane, in the county of Dane, shall constitute an assembly district.

The village and town of Madison, and the towns of Blooming Grove, Burk, Westport, Vienna, and Windsor, in the county of Dane, shall constitute an assembly district.

The towns of White Oak Springs, Benton and New Diggings, in the county of La Fayette, shall constitute an assembly district.

The towns of Shullsburg, Monticello, Gratiot, Wayne and Wiota, in the county of La Fayette, shall constitute an assembly district.

The towns of Elk Grove, Belmont, Kendall, Center, Willow Springs, Fayette and Argyle, in the county of La Fayette, shall constitute an assembly district.

The town of Watertown, in the county of Jefferson, shall constitute an assembly district.

The towns of Waterloo, Milford, Lake Mills and Oakland, in the county of Jefferson, shall constitute an assembly district.

The towns of Jefferson and Koshkonong, in the county of Jefferson, shall constitute an assembly district.

The towns of Ixonia, Concord, Farmington and Aztalan, in the county of Jefferson, shall constitute an assembly district.

The towns of Hebron, Sullivan, Cold Spring and Palmyra, [in the county of Jefferson,] shall constitute an assembly district.

The towns of Highland, Dodgeville, Ridgeway, Arena, Wyoming, Pulaski and Clyde, in the county of Iowa, shall constitute an assembly district.

The towns of Mineral Point, Mifflin, Lyndon and Walderich, in the county of Iowa, shall constitute an assembly district.

The county of Richland shall constitute an assembly district.

The towns of Hazel Green, Jamestown and Smeltzer, in the county of Grant, shall constitute an assembly district.

The towns of Potosi, Paris and Harrington, in the county of Grant, shall constitute an assembly district.

The towns of Platteville, Lima, Clifton, Muscoda and Wingville, in the county of Grant, shall constitute an assembly district.

The towns of Fennimore, 'Highland and Lancaster, in the county of Grant, shall constitute an assembly district.

The towns of Waterloo, Beetown, Patch Grove and Cassville, in the county of Grant, shall constitute an assembly district.

The counties of Bad Ax and Crawford, shall constitute an assembly district.

The counties of La Crosse and Chippewa, shall constitute an assembly district.

The counties of St. Croix and La Pointe, shall constitute an assembly district.

The towns of Whitewater, Richland, and La Grange, in the county of Walworth, shall constitute an assembly district.

The towns of Sugar Creek, La Fayette and Troy, in the county of Walworth, shall constitute an assembly district.

The towns of East Troy and Spring Prairie, in the county of Walworth, shall constitute an assembly district.

The towns of Elkhorn, Geneva and Hudson, in the county of Walworth, shall constitute an assembly district.

The towns of Delavan, Darien and Sharon, in the county of Walworth, shall constitute an assembly district.

The towns of Walworth, Lynn and Bloomfield, in the county of Walworth, shall constitute an assembly district.

The towns of Beloit, Turtle and Clinton, in the county of Rock, sall constitute an assembly district.

The towns of Milton, Harmony, Lima, Johnstown, Bradford and La prairie, in the county of Rock, shall constitute an assembly district.

The towns of Janesville, Rock, Centre and Fulton, in the county of Rock shall constitute an assembly district.

The towns of Porter, Union, Magnolia, Spring Valley, Plymouth, Newark and Avon, in the county of Rock, shall constitute an assembly district.

The towns of Ceresco, Metomen, Alto, Waupun, Spring Vale and Rosendale, in the county of Fond du Lac, shall constitute an assembly district.

The towns of Byron, Eden, Osceola, Ashford and Auburn, in the county of Fond du Lac, shall constitute an assembly district.

The towns of Eldorado, Lamartine, Oakfield, Fond du Lac and Friendship, and the city of Fond du Lac, in the county of Fond du Lac, shall constitute an assembly district.

The towns of Calumet, Forrest, Taycheedah, Kossuth and Empire, in the county of Fond du Lac, shall constitute an assembly district.

Townships seventeen and eighteen, ranges fourteen, fifteen, sixteen and seventeen, in the county of Winnebago, shall constitute an assembly district.

Townships nineteen and twenty, in ranges fourteen, fifteen, sixteen and seventeen, in Winnebago county, shall constitute an assembly district.

The towns of Leroy, Lomira, Williamstown and Theresa, in the county of Dodge, shall constitute an assembly district.

The towns of Hubbard, Hermon, Hustisford and Rubicon, in the county of Dodge, shall constitute an assembly district.

The towns of Emmett, Lebanon and Ashippun, in the county of Dodge, shall constitute an assembly district.

The towns of Elba, Lowell, Clyman, Portland and Shields, in the county of Dodge, shall constitute an assembly district.

The towns of Fox Lake, Trenton, Westford, Calamus and Beaver Dam, [in the county of Dodge,] shall constitute an assembly district.

The towns of Chester, Burnette and Oak Grove, in the county of Dodge, shall constitute an assembly district.

The towns of Berlin, Brooklyn, Pleasant Valley, Middleton, Mackford, Albany and Green Lake, in the county of Marquette and the county of Waushara, shall constitute an assembly district.

All that portion of Marquette county being west of the range line between ranges ten and eleven east and the towns of Marquette and Kingston, in the county of Marquette, shall constitute an assembly district.

The counties of Sauk and Adams shall constitute an assembly district.

The county of Green shall constitute an assembly district.

The towns of Fort Winnebago, Port Hope, Marcellon, Scott, Randolph, Portage Prairie, Spring Vale and Wyocena, in the county of Columbia, shall constitute an assembly district.

The towns of Columbus, Fountain Prairie, Hampden, Otsego, Leeds, Lowville, Lodi, Dekorra, West Point and Caledonia, in the county of Columbia, shall constitute an assembly district.

———

SEC. 2. At the general election in November, A. D. one thousand eight hundred and fifty-two, there shall be elected in the fourth, tenth, and eighteenth senate districts, each, as above described, a state senator, whose term of office shall expire on the day preceding the first Monday in January, A. D. one thousand eight hundred and fifty-four.

J. McM. SHAFTER,
Speaker of the Assembly.

E. B. DEAN, JR.,
President pro. tem. of the Senate.

Approved, April 19, 1852.

LEONARD J. FARWELL.

10

GOVERNORS OF THE TERRITORY AND STATE OF WISCONSIN.

BY WHOM APPOINTED AND WHEN ELECTED.

Henry Dodge, appointed by Andrew Jackson,   April 30, 1836.
James Duane Doty,   do.   John Tyler, . .   Sept. 30, 1841.
Nathaniel P. Talmadge, do.   do.   . .   June 21, 1844.
Henry Dodge,   do.   James K. Polk, .   April 8, 1845.
Nelson Dewey, elected . . . .   May 8, 1848.
Nelson Dewey, re-elected . . . .   Nov. 1849.
Leonard J. Farwell, elected . . . .   Nov. 4, 1851.

LIEUTENANT-GOVERNORS OF THE STATE OF WISCONSIN.

WHEN ELECTED.

John E. Holmes, elected . . . . .   May 8, 1848.
Samuel W. Beall, elected , ...   Nov. 1849.
Timothy Burns, elected . . . . .   Nov. 4, 1851.

CONGRESSIONAL DISTRICTS OF THE STATE OF WISCONSIN.

FIRST DISTRICT.

Milwaukee.	Walworth.	Racine.
Waukesha.		

SECOND DISTRICT.

Rock.	Dane.	Crawford.
Green.	Sauk.	Chippewa.
La Fayette.	Adams.	St. Croix.
Grant.	Portage.	La Point.
Iowa.	Richland.	

THIRD DISTRICT.

Washington.	Winnebago.	Columbia.
Sheboygan.	Calumet.	Dodge.
Manitowoc.	Fond du Lac.	Jefferson.
Brown.	Marquette.	

LIST OF COUNTY OFFICERS

IN THE SEVERAL COUNTIES OF THE STATE OF WISCONSIN, ELECTED
ON THE SECOND DAY OF NOVEMBER, A. D. 1852.

ADAMS . . . . .

BAD AX . . . . James Bailey, Sheriff.
William F. Terhune, Clerk of the Court.

BROWN . . . . . John Last, Clerk of the Court.
E. H. Ellis, Register of Deeds.
O. B. Graves, Sheriff.

CALUMET . . . . Charles Greening, Clerk of the Court.
L. P. Fowler, Register of Deeds.
J. S. Hammer, Sheriff.

CHIPPEWA . . .

CRAWFORD . . . Ira B. Brunson, Register of Deeds.
Leander Le Clerc, Sheriff.
Ira B. Brunson, Clerk of Circuit Court.

COLUMBIA . . . James Delany, Jr , Clerk of Circuit Court.
Perry Lee, Sheriff.
William Owen, Register of Deeds.

DANE . . . . . . Willet S. Main, Sheriff.
             John B. Sweat, Register of Deeds.
             Charles Lumm, Clerk of Circuit Court.

DOOR . . . . . .

FOND DU LAC . Robert Jenkinson, Sheriff.
             Rudolph Ebert, Register of Deeds.
             John J. Driggs, Clerk of Circuit Court.

GRANT . . . . . William McGonigal, Sheriff.
             Nathaniel W. Kendall, Clerk of Circuit Court.
             George H. Cox, Register of Deeds.

GREEN . . . . . John Moore, Sheriff.
             Noah Phelps, Clerk of Circuit Court.
             James L. Powell, Register of Deeds.

IOWA . . . . . . C. N. Menford, Sheriff.
             N. B. Boyden, Register of Deeds.
             James Hutchinson, Clerk of Circuit Court.

JEFFERSON . . . Austin Kellogg, Sheriff.
             Royal Tyler, Register of Deeds.
             Walter H. Besley, Clerk of Circuit Court.

KENOSHA . . . . Patrick Cosgrove, Sheriff.
             Samuel T. Brand, Register of Deeds.
             Oscar F. Dana, Clerk of Circuit Court.

LA CROSS . . . . A. Eldred, Sheriff.
             Robert Looney, Clerk of Court.
             C. A. Stevens, Register of Deeds.

LA FAYETTE . . David W. Kyle, Clerk of Circuit Court.
             Peter C. Meloy, Sheriff.
             Elias Slothoneer, Register of Deeds.

LA POINTE . . . Robert D. Boyd, Clerk of Circuit Court.
             Robert D. Boyd, Register of Deeds.

MARATHON . . . Thomas Minton, Sheriff.
             Asa Lawrence, Clerk of Circuit Court.

MANITOWOC . . Fred. Solomon, Register of Deeds.
             D. H. Van Valkenburgh, Sheriff.

MARQUETTE. . . James C. Potter, Sheriff.
             Dominie Devenna, Clerk of Court.
             J. Edmund Millard, Register of Deeds.

MILWAUKEE . . Hermon L. Page, Sheriff.
             Matthew Keenan, Clerk of Circuit Court.
             Charles J. Kern, Register of Deeds.

OUTAGAMIE . . . Almeron B. Everts, Sheriff.
             Henry S. Eggleston, Clerk of Court.
             Julius S. Buck, Register of Deeds.

OCONTO . . . . . William Bronqueet, Register of Deeds.

PORTAGE . . . . Aaron Drake, Sheriff.
             John Stump, Register of Deeds.

RACINE . . . . . Timothy D. Mooris, Sheriff.
             Chatfield H. Parsons, Register of Deeds.
             Samuel G. Knight, Clerk of Circuit Court.

RICHLAND . . . Robert C. Hawkins, Sheriff.
             A. B. Slaughter, Clerk of Circuit Court.
             Charles M. McCorkle, Register of Deeds.

ROCK . . . . . . William H. Howard, Sheriff.
             Samuel A. Martin, Register of Deeds.
             George W. Crabb, Clerk of Circuit Court.

ST. CROIX . . . William R. Anderson, Register of Deeds.
A. S. Foull, Sheriff.

SAUK . . . . . . Daniel Munson, Sheriff.
Edwin P. Spencer, Register of Deeds.
George Mertons, Clerk of Court.

SHEBOYGAN . . John D. Murphy, Sheriff.
Alexander H. Edwards, Clerk of Court.
Charles Adolphi, Register of Deeds.

WALWORTH . . William H. Petit, Clerk of Court.
J. C. Crum, Sheriff.
John Perry, Register of Deeds.

WASHINGTON . . Lion Silvermore, Sheriff.
Adam Shauty, Register of Deeds.
Lafayette Towsley, Clerk of Circuit Court.

WAUKESHA . . . Charles B. Ellis, Sheriff.
William R. Williams, Register of Deeds.
Lemuel White, Clerk of Circuit Court.

WAUPACCA . . .

WAUSHARA . . . Nathaniel Boyington, Sheriff.
Jacob S. Bugle, Register of Deeds.
Allyn Boardman, Clerk of Circuit Court.

WINNEBAGO . . Edwin R. Rowly, Register of Deeds.
Edwin R. Baldwin, Clerk of Circuit Court.
Alexander F. David, Sheriff.

80

JUDICIAL DEPARTMENT.

JUDGES OF NEW SUPREME COURT.

Edward V. Whiton, Chief Justice.
Abram D. Smith, }
Samuel Crawford, } Associates.

Salaries of Judges of Supreme Court, $2,000 per year each.

CIRCUIT JUDGES IN THE STATE.

Judge of 1st Circuit, Edward V. Whiton . . . . Salary $1,500
    2d do.   Levi Hubbell : . . . . . . do.
    3d do.   Charles H. Larrabee . . . do.
    4th do.   Timothy C. Howe . . . . . . do.
    5th do.   Montgomery M. Cothren . do.
    6th do.   Wiram Knowlton . . . . . do.

EXECUTIVE DEPARTMENT.

STATE OFFICERS.

Governor . . . . Leonard J. Farwell . . Salary $1,250
Lieutenant Governor . . . . Timothy Burns . . . . .
Secretary of State . . . . . Charles D. Robinson . do. 1,200
State Treasurer . . . . Edward H. Janssen . . do. 800
Attorney General . . . . . Experience Estabrook . do. 800
State Super. of Instruction . Azel P. Ladd . . . . . do. 1,000
Bank Comptroller . . . . James S. Baker . . . . do. 2,000

OFFICERS OF WISCONSIN MILITIA.

Leonard J. Farwell, Commander-in-Chief, Madison.

GENERAL STAFF.

Benj. F. Hopkins, Madison,
C. C. Washburne, Mineral Point,
Coles Bashford, Oshkosh,
Charles Clement, Kenosha,
} Governor's Aids.

William L. Utley,	Racine,	Adjut. General, Salary $300.
David Atwood,	Madison,	Quarter-Master General.
James B. Martin,	Milwaukee,	Pay-Master General.
James Richardson,	Madison,	Commissary General.
John W. Hunt, M. D.	Madison,	Surgeon General.
N. Bishop Eddy,	Madison,	Judge Advocate General.
William Dudley,	Madison,	Military Secretary.

COMMISSIONERS OF PUBLIC WORKS.

Andrew Proudfit. Peter H. Prame. William Richardson.

COMMISSIONER OF STATE PRISON.

Henry Brown.

STATE LIBRARIAN.

William Dudley . . . . Salary $600.

PRIVATE SECRETARY OF GOVERNOR.

Harlow S. Orton . . . . Salary $600.

REGENTS OF WISCONSIN UNIVERSITY.

John H. Lathrop.	Eleazor Root.	E. B. Wolcott.
Simeon Mills.	Nath. W. Dean.	James B. Ruggles.
John H. Rountree.	Hiram Barber.	A. Hyatt Smith.
Rufus King.	John Banister.	Godfrey Aigner.

11

OFFICERS OF BOARD OF REGENTS.

Chairman Executive Committee . J. H. Lathrop.

Building Committee . . . . J. H. Lathrop.

Treasurer . . . . Simeon Mills.

Auditing Committee . . . . . . {J. H. Lathrop.
{J. T. Clarke.

Commissioner . . . . Simeon Mills.

LEGISLATURE.

SENATORS BY DISTRICTS.

1st District, H. N. Smith.	14th District, Alva Stewart.
2d do. James S. Alban.	15th do. Levi Sterling.
3d do. A. M. Blair.	16th do. Joel C. Squires.
4th do. B. S. Weil.	17th do. Ezra Miller.
5th do. E. M. Hunter.	18th do. J. R. Briggs, Jr.
6th do. D. C. Reed.	19th do. Benjamin Allen.
7th do. J. W. Cary.	20th do. Bert. Pinckney.
8th do. J. R. Sharpstein.	21st do. Coles Bashford.
9th do. Geo. R. McLane.	22d do. Judson Prentice.
10th do. M. H. Bovee.	23d do. David S. Vittum.
11th do. T. T. Whittlesey.	24th do. Thos. S. Bowen.
12th do. E. Wakely.	25th do. James T. Lewis.
13th do. Charles Dunn.	

MEMBERS OF ASSEMBLY BY DISTRICTS.

ADAMS and SAUK COUNTIES—Charles Armstrong.

BROWN, KEWAUNEE and DOOR—Randall Wilcox.

BAD AX and CRAWFORD—H. A. Wright.

CALUMET—J. Robinson.

CHIPPEWA and LA CROSSE—A. D. La Due.

COLUMBIA—O. D. Coleman and J. Q. Adams.

DANE—Matthew Roche, H. Barnes, H. L. Foster, P. C. Burdick, and S. W. Field.

DODGE—Whitman Sayles, W. M. Dennis, P. Kelly, John W. Davis, Edwin Hillyer, and E. N. Foster.

FOND DU LAC—I. S. Tallmadge, Charles D. Gage, Querin Loehr and N. M. Donaldson.

GRANT—J. E. Dodge, J. A. Barber, H. E. Block, H. D. York, and T. Hayes.

GREEN—Thomas Fenton.

IOWA—H. Maddin and P. W. Thomas.

JEFFERSON—Patrick Rogan, W. W. Woodman, D. Powers, J. E. Holmes and J. H. Ostrander.

KENOSHA—J. McKesson and C. L. Sholes.

LAFAYETTE—Eli Robinson, P. B. Simpson and Nathan Olmstead.

MARQUETTE and WAUSHARA—Ezra Wheeler.

MARQUETTE—E. B. Kelsey.

MILWAUKEE—H. Haertel, E. McGarry, H. L. Palmer, R. Carlile, H. C. West, J. Myers, J. H. Tweedy, W. A. Hawkins and E. Chase.

MANITOWOC—E. Ricker.

OUTAGAMIE, WAUPACA and OCONTO—A. Realey.

PORTAGE—G. W. Cate.

RACINE—H. T. Sanders, W. H. Roe, Thomas West, and Philo Belden.

RICHLAND—Henry Conner.

ROCK—C. Stevens, H. Stebbins, W. D. Murray and H. Holmes.

SHEBOYGAN—C. B. Coleman and D. Taylor.

ST. CROIX and LA POINTE—O. T. Maxson.

WALWORTH—John Bell, James Lauderdale, O. T. Bartlett, T. H. Fellows, Joseph W. Seaver, and T. W. Hill.

WASHINGTON—C. E. Chamberlain, C. Schutte, W. P. Barnes and J. W. Porter.

WAUKESHA—Orson Reed, E. Lees, W. D. Bacon and Elisha Pearl.

WINNEBAGO—Curtis Reed and Lucas M. Miller.

MEMBERS AND OFFICERS OF THE SENATE.

Names.	Town.	County.	Age.	State of Nativity.	Occupation.	Years in State.	Boarding Place.	Senate District.
MEMBERS.								
Horatio N. Smith	Plymouth	Sheboygan	32	Vermont	Farmer	6	Fairchild	1st
James S. Alban	Plover	Portage	43	Ohio	Lawyer	16	Reynolds	2d
Andrew M. Blair	Port Washington	Washington	36	Vermont	Lawyer	3	Main	3d
Baruch S. Weil	West Bend	Washington	50	Strasburg, France	Farmer	8	Varney	4th
Edward M. Hunter	Milwaukee	Milwaukee	26	New York	Lawyer	4	Beriah Brown	5th
Duncan C. Reed	Milwaukee	Milwaukee	37	Vermont	Engineer	12	American	6th
John W. Cary	Racine	Racine	35	Vermont	Lawyer	3	Hood	7th
John R. Sharpstein	Kenosha	Kenosha	29	New York	Lawyer	6	Hood	8th
George R. McLane	Delafield	Waukesha	33	Delaware	Lawyer	5	American	9th
Marvin H. Bovee	Eagle	Waukesha	26	New York	Farmer	9	Varney	10th
Thomas T. Whittlesey	Pleasant Branch	Dane	52	Connecticut	Farmer	7	Seth Van Bergen	11th
Eleazer Wakeley	Whitewater	Walworth	40	New York	Lawyer	7	American	12th
Charles Dunn	Belmont	Lafayette	53	Kentucky	Lawyer	17	Kellogg	13th
Alva Stewart	Fort Atkinson	Jefferson	31	New York	Lawyer	-5	Atwood	14th
Levi Sterling	Mineral Point	Iowa	47	Kentucky	Farmer	25	American	15th
Joel C. Squires	Lancaster	Grant	31	Ohio	Carpenter	12	American	16th
Ezra Miller	Magnolia	Rock	40	New York	Farmer	6	American	17th
John R. Briggs, Jr.	Beloit	Rock	30	Massachusetts	Printer	4	Atwood	18th
Benjamin Allen	Hudson	St. Croix	39	Vermont	Lawyer	3	Kellogg	19th
Bertine Pinckney	Rosendale	Fond du Lac	29	New York	Farmer	6	Atwood	20th
Coles Bashford	Algoma	Winnebago	35	New York	Lawyer	2	Atwood	21st
Judson Prentice	Oak Grove	Dodge	43	New Hampshire	Surveyor	9	D Hol.	22d
David S. Vittum	Baraboo	Sauk	30	Vermont	Lawyer	1	Mrs. Van Bergen	23d
Thomas S. Bowen	Clarno	Green	44	Vermont	Farmer	17	Badger House	24th
James T. Lewis	Columbus	Columbia	33	New York	Lawyer	8	Badger House	25th
OFFICERS.								
Timothy Burns, President	La Crosse	La Crosse	33	Ireland	Farmer	15	American	
J.K. Williams, Chief Clerk	Shullsburg	La Fayette	30	Pennsylvania	Lawyer	7	Badger House	
Geo. H. Paul, Assist. Clerk	Kenosha	Kenosha	26	Vermont	Editor	2	Major Hood	
Thos. Hood, Serg't-at-Arms	Madison	Dane	36	Ohio	Lawyer	3	Mrs. Hood	

RULES AND ORDERS OF THE SENATE.

RULE 1. The Lieutenant Governor of the state, by the eighth section of the fifth article of the Constitution, is constituted, ex-officio, the President of the Senate; shall, therefore, when present take the chair at the hour fixed for the meeting of the Senate, when he shall immediately call the members to order, who shall thereupon take their seats, and continue with their heads uncovered while the Senate remains in session; the clerk shall call the roll of members, and as soon as a majority is present, the journal of the preceding day shall be read, to the end that any mistake may be corrected.

RULE 2. The President shall preserve order and decorum; he may speak to points of order in preference to other members, rising from his seat for that purpose; and shall decide questions of order, subject to an appeal to the senate by any member.

RULE 3. The President shall have the right to name any member to perform the duties of the chair temporarily, who shall be invested, during such time, with all the powers of the President; but no member shall be excused from voting on any question by reason of his occupying the chair; nor shall such substitute's authority as presiding officer extend beyond a daily adjournment of the senate.

RULE 4. In the absence or inability of the President, except as provided in rule three, the senate shall appoint a President pro tempore, who shall possess all the powers and prerogatives of the President of the senate for the time being.

RULE 5. Whenever the senate determines to go into committee of the whole, the President shall name one of the members as chairman, who shall for the time being be invested with all the authority of presiding officer of the senate.

RULE 6. The President shall appoint all committees unless otherwise directed; he shall sign all acts, memorials, addresses and resolutions; and all writs, warrants and subpœnas that may be issued by the senate, shall be signed by him and attested by the clerk.

RULE 7. Whenever any disturbance or disorderly conduct shall occur in the lobby, the President (or chairman of the committee of the whole) shall have the power to cause the same to be cleared of all persons except the members and officers of the senate.

RULE 8. Questions may be stated by the President while sitting, but he shall rise to put a question, and shall use this form, viz: "As many as are of the opinion that (as the question may be) will say Aye;" and after the affirmative voice is expressed, "as many as are of a different opinion, will say No." If the President doubt as to the voice of the majority, or a division be called for, the senate shall divide—those in the affirmative of the question shall first rise and be counted; and those in the negative shall then rise in like manner and be counted; and if there still be doubt, or a count be called for, the President shall appoint two tellers, one from each side, to make the count and report the result to the President, who shall declare it to the senate.

RULE 9. A majority of all the members elected to the senate, must be present to constitute a quorum for the transaction of ordinary business; a smaller number, however, can adjourn from time to time, and have power to compel the attendance of absent members.

RULE 10. No member or officer of the senate, unless from illness or other cause he shall be unable to attend, shall absent himself from the sessions of the senate during an entire day, without first having obtained leave of absence.

RULE 11. Any committee required or entitled to report upon a subject referred to them, may make a majority and minority report; any member of such committee, dissenting in whole or in part from either the conclusion or the reasoning of both the majority and the minority, shall be entitled to present to the senate a brief statement of his reasons for such dissent, which, if decorous in its language and respectful to the senate, shall be entered on the journal in connexion with the majority and minority reports.

RULE 12. A clerk shall be elected at the commencement of each session, to hold his office at the pleasure of the senate; he shall keep a correct journal of the daily proceedings of the senate, and perform such other duties as may be assigned to him; he shall superintend the recording of the journal of proceedings, the engrossing, enrolling, transcribing and copying of bills, resolutions, &c.; shall permit no records nor papers belonging to the senate to be taken out of his custody, otherwise than in the regular course of business; shall report any missing papers to the notice of the President; and generally shall perform, under the direction of the President, all duties pertaining to his office as clerk.

RULE 13. A sergeant-at-arms shall be elected at the commencement of each session, to hold his office at the pleasure of the senate. It shall be his duty to execute all orders of the President or senate, and to perform all duties they may assign to him connected with the police and good order of the senate chamber; to exercise a supervision over the ingress and egress of all persons to and from the chamber, to see that messages, &c., are promptly executed, that the requisite fires are kept up during the appropriate season, and to perform all other services pertaining to the post of sergeant-at-arms.

RULE 14. The following standing committees shall be appointed by the President, at the commencement of each session, unless otherwise directed by the senate. The committee on the judiciary shall consist of five members, and the other committees of three members each.

1st. On the Judiciary.
2nd. On Finance.
3rd. On Education, School and University Lands.
4th. On Incorporations.
5th. On Claims.
6th. On Internal Improvements.
7th. On Roads, Bridges and Ferries.
8th. On Town and County Organization.
9th. On the Militia.
10th. On Privileges and Elections.
11th. On Agriculture and Manufactures.
12th. On the Expiration and Re-enactment of Laws, &c.
13th. On Legislative Expenditures.
14th. On State Affairs.
15th. On Public Printing.
16th. On Banks and Banking.
17th. On Engrossed Bills.
18th. On Contingent Expenditures.
19th. On Public Lands.
20th. On Enrolled Bills.

RULE 15. Reporters for newspapers can have seats assigned them by the President, within the bar of the chamber, for the purpose of taking down the proceedings, but not so as to interfere with the convenience of the senate. The governor, lieutenant governor, secretary of state, treasurer, attorney general, senators and ex-senators, and members of congress, judges of any courts, members and ex-members of state legislatures, and members of the assembly of this state, and all editors of newspapers in the state, may be admitted to seats within the bar of the senate.

12

RULE 16. ˙ After the journal shall have been read, and an opportunity given to correct it, the order of business shall be as follows, viz:

1. Letters, petitions, memorials, remonstrances, and accompanying documents, may be presented and referred.

2. Resolutions may be offered and considered, notice of leave to introduce bills may be given, and bills may be introduced on leave granted.

3. Reports of committees may be made and considered, first from standing committees, and next from select committees.

4. Messages and other executive communications.

5. Messages from the assembly, and amendments proposed by the assembly to bills from the senate.

6. Bills and resolutions from the assembly on their second reading.

7. Bills on their third reading.

8. Bills ready for a third reading.

9. Bills reported for a committee of the whole.

10. Bills in which a committee of the whole has made progress, and obtained leave to sit again.

11. Bills not yet considered in committee of the whole.

RULE 17. Bills of a public nature shall always take precedence of private bills.

RULE 18. When any member is about to speak in debate, or deliver any matter to the senate, he shall rise from his seat and respectfully address himself to " Mr. President," and shall confine himself to the question under consideration, and avoid personalities.

RULE 19. Whenever any member is called to order, he shall sit down until it be determined whether he is in order or not, except he be permitted to explain; and if a member be called to order for words spoken in debate, the exceptionable words shall be taken down in writing immediately.

RULE 20. When two or more members happen to rise at the same time, the President shall name the member who is first to speak; but the member first rising shall at all times be entitled to the floor.

RULE 21. No member shall speak more than twice on the same question during the same day; nor more than once on a motion for commitment, without leave of the senate.

RULE 22. Whilst the President is putting any question or addressing the senate, no member shall walk out of or across the room, nor entertain private discourse; nor whilst a member is speaking, shall pass between him and the chair. No member or other person shall visit or remain by the clerk's table whilst the ayes and noes are being called, or the ballots counted,

RULE 23. No member shall vote on any question in any case where he was not within the chamber of the senate when the question was put, unless by leave of the senate; nor shall any member be counted, upon a division and count of the senate, who shall be without the chamber at the time.

RULE 24. Every member who may be within the senate chamber when the question was put, shall give his vote, unless the senate for special reasons shall excuse him. All motions to excuse a member from voting, shall be made before the senate divides, or before the call of the ayes and noes is commenced. And any member wishing to be excused from voting, may make a brief verbal statement of the reasons for making such request, and the question shall then be taken without further debate.

RULE 25. When a motion is made and seconded, it shall be stated by the president, or, being in writing, it shall be handed to the chair, and read aloud before debated.

RULE 26. Every motion shall be reduced to writing, if the President or any member desire it.

RULE 27. After a motion is stated by the President, or read by the clerk, it shall be deemed to be in the possession of the senate, but may be withdrawn or altered at any time before a decision or amendment.

RULE 28. When a question is under debate, no motion shall be received unless to adjourn, to lay on the table, for the previous question, to postpone to a day certain, to commit, to amend, or to postpone indefinitely; and these several motions shall have precedence in the order in which they stand arranged. A motion to postpone to a day certain, or to postpone indefinitely, being decided, shall not again be allowed on the same day, or at the same stage of the bill or proposition. A motion to strike out the enacting words of a bill shall have precedence of a motion to amend, and if carried, shall be equivalent to the rejection of the bill.

RULE 29. A motion to adjourn, shall be always in order; that and the motion to lay on the table shall be decided without debate.

RULE 30. The previous question shall be in this form: "Shall the main question be now put?" It shall only be admitted when demanded by a majority of the members present, and until it is decided shall preclude amendment and further debate of the main question. When on taking the previous question, the senate shall decide that the previous question shall not now be put, the main question shall be considered as still remaining under debate. The "main question" shall be on the the passage of the bill, resolution, or other matter under consideration. And in cases where there shall be pending amendments, the question shall first be taken upon amendments in their order, and without further debate or amendment. On a motion for the previous question, and prior to the main question being put, a call of the senate shall be in order. No debate shall be permitted on a previous question; and all incidental questions of order arising after a motion is made for the previous question, and pending such motion, shall be decided, whether on appeal or otherwise, without debate.

RULE 31. When a motion or question has been once put and carried in the affirmative or negative, it shall be in order for any member who voted in the majority, or when the senate is equally divided, for a member who voted in the negative, to move for a re-consideration thereof on the same or succeeding day; and such motion shall take precedence of all other questions except to adjourn. A motion to reconsider being put and lost, shall not be renewed.

RULE 32. Any member may call for a division of the question, when the same will admit of it. A motion to strike out and insert shall be deemed to be indivisible. A motion to strike out being lost, shall not preclude an amendment, nor a motion to strike out and insert.

RULE 33. In presenting a petition, memorial, remonstrance or other communication, addressed to the senate or assembly, the member shall only state the general purport of it.

RULE 34. A member offering a resolution, or an amendment to a bill, resolution or memorial, shall first read the same in his place, before presenting it to the President; and every petition, memorial, remonstrance, resolution, bill and report of committee shall be endorsed with its appropriate title; and immediately under the endorsement the name of the member presenting the same shall be written.

RULE 35. Any two members may make a call of the senate and require absent members to be sent for, but a call of the senate cannot be made after the voting has commenced; and the call of the senate being ordered, and the absentees noted, the doors shall be closed and no member permitted to leave the room until the report of the sergeant-at-arms be received and acted upon, or further proceedings in the call be suspended. Previous to the reception of such report, further proceedings in the call shall not be suspended, except by a vote of two-thirds of the members present.

Rule 36. The rules observed in the senate shall govern, as far as practicable, the proceedings in committee of the whole, except that a member may speak oftener than twice on the same subject, and that a call for the ayes and noes, or for the previous question, cannot be made in committee.

Rule 37. Amendments made in committee of the whole shall be entered on a separate piece of paper, and so reported to the senate by the chairman, standing in his place; which amendments shall not be read by the President, unless required by one or more of the members. Amendments and other propositions reported by the committee of the whole shall be disposed of in the same manner as if proposed in the senate.

Rule 38. All bills and resolutions shall be introduced by motion for leave or upon the reports of committees. Members before introducing a bill shall always give one day's notice of a motion to bring it in, and when introduced, it shall be endorsed with the name of the member or the committee.

Rule 39. Every bill or joint resolution requiring the approval of the governor, shall receive three several readings, previous to its passage; the first reading shall be at length, and no bill shall receive a second and third reading on the same day.

Rule 40. No bill or joint resolution shall be committed or amended until it has been twice read. If objections are made to the bill on its first reading the question shall be, "Shall the bill be rejected?" If no objection be made or the question to reject be lost, the bill shall go to its second reading.

Rule 41. All bills and joint resolutions, requiring the approval of the governor, shall, on a second reading be considered in committee of the whole, before they shall be acted upon by the senate; and those originating in the senate, except resolutions not requiring the approval of the governor, before being considered in committee of the whole, shall be printed, unless otherwise ordered by the senate.

RULE 42. One hundred and fifty copies of every bill, joint resolution or memorial, shall be printed, after the second reading, unless otherwise ordered. And all bills, resolutions and amendments, after being printed, shall remain at least one day on the files before being considered.

RULE 43. No more than three bills originating in the senate shall be committed to the same committee of the whole.

RULE 44. The final question upon the second reading of every bill or other paper originating in the senate, and requiring three readings previous to being passed, shall be "Shall it be engrossed and read the third time?" and upon every such bill or paper originating in the assembly, "Shall it be read a third time?"

RULE 45. No amendments shall be received on third reading, except to fill blanks, without the unanimous consent of the senate. In filling blanks, the largest sum, longest time, the greatest distance shall be first taken.

RULE 46. A bill or resolution may be committed at any time previous to its passage; and if any amendment be reported upon such commitment, by any other than a committee of the whole, it shall be again read a second time, considered in committee of the whole, and the question for third reading and passage again put.

RULE 47. Every bill, joint resolution or memorial, originating in the senate, shall be carefully engrossed before being transmitted to the assembly for concurrence.

RULE 48. Immediately after the passage of any bill or other paper, to which the concurrence of the assembly is to be asked, it shall be the duty of the clerk to transmit the same to the assembly, unless some member of the senate shall make a motion to reconsider the vote by which the senate passed such bill or other paper, in which case the clerk shall not transmit said bill or other paper, until the motion to reconsider has been put; and on the concurrence in anv bill or other paper of the assembly by the senate, or on the concurrence or disagreement in any vote of the house, it shall also be the duty of the clerk to notify the assembly thereof.

RULE 49. Memorials to congress, to the president of the United States, or the head of either of the departments, shall be considered in committee of the whole before being adopted.

RULE 50. It shall be competent for any member when a question is being taken, to call for the ayes and noes, which shall be inserted on the journal. A call for the ayes and noes cannot be interrupted in any manner whatever.

RULE 51. Committees shall not absent themselves from the senate by reason of their appointment, without special leave for that purpose be first obtained.

RULE 52. It shall be in order for the committee on enrollment to report at any time.

RULE 53. The proceedings of the senate on executive business shall be kept in a separate book of record, to be provided by the chief clerk of the senate, and published with the proceedings of the senate. When an amendment to the constitution, or any bill requiring the concurrence of more than a majority of senators present is under consideration, the concurrence of only a majority of the senators present, shall be requisite to decide any question for amendments or extending to the merits, being short of the final question.

RULE 54. The rules of parliamentary practice, comprised in Jefferson's Manual, shall govern the senate in all cases to which they are applicable, and in which they are not inconsistent with these rules and the orders of the senate, and the joint rules and orders of the senate and assembly. Upon the final passage of any bill or proposition in which the concurrence of more than a majority of senators present is required by the constitution of this state, the question shall be taken by ayes and noes, which shall be entered at large on the journal, and it shall be the duty of the chief clerk to certify on the back of every such bill or proposition the number of senators voting for and against the passage of the same.

RULE 55. The President is authorized to administer all oaths prescribed by the foregoing rules.

RULE 56. The standing hour for the daily meeting of the Senate, shall be ten o'clock in the morning, until the Senate direct otherwise.

RULE 57. No standing rule or order of the Senate shall be rescinded or changed without one day's notice of the motion therefor. Nor shall any rule be rescinded, changed or suspended, except by a vote of at least two-thirds of the members present.

STANDING COMMITTEES OF THE SENATE.

JUDICIARY—Messrs. Dunn, Wakeley, Stewart, Blair and Lewis.

EDUCATION, SCHOOL AND UNIVERSITY LANDS—Messrs. Wakeley, Alban and Whittlesey.

FINANCE—Messrs. Whittlesey, Miller and Smith.

CLAIMS—Messrs. Smith, McLane and Prentice.

INCORPORATIONS—Messrs. Sharpstein, Reed and Alban.

INTERNAL IMPROVEMENTS—Messrs. Hunter, Pinckney and Vittum.

ROADS AND BRIDGES—Messrs. Sterling, Brown and Bovee.

TOWN AND COUNTY ORGANIZATION—Messrs. Bovee, Bashford and Weil.

MILITIA—Messrs. Pinckney, Briggs and Bowen.

AGRICULTURE AND MANUFACTURES—Messrs. McLane, Prentice and Dunn.

EXPIRATION AND RE-ENACTMENT OF LAWS—Messrs. Lewis, Reed and Hunter.

LEGISLATIVE EXPENDITURES—Messrs. Alban, Vittum and Sharpstein.

STATE AFFAIRS—Messrs. Blair, Squires and Miller.

PUBLIC PRINTING—Messrs. Miller, Briggs and Carey.

CONTINGENT EXPENDITURES—Messrs. Allen, Smith and Bashford.

BANKS AND BANKING—Messrs. Carey, Whittlesey and Dunn.

PUBLIC LANDS—Messrs. Vittum, Prentice and McLane.

ENROLLED BILLS—Messrs. Squires, Bovee and Carey.

ENGROSSED BILLS—Messrs. Stewart, Blair and Hunter.

PRIVILEGES AND ELECTIONS—Messrs. Weil, Pinckney and Sterling.

RULES AND ORDERS OF THE ASSEMBLY.

I. The assembly shall choose, viva voce, one of their own members to occupy the chair. He shall be styled Speaker of the assembly. He shall hold his office during one session of the assembly. He shall take the chair at the hour to which the house is adjourned, and call the members to order, and if a quorum be present he shall direct the minutes of the preceding day to be read, and mistakes, if any, corrected. He shall preserve order and decorum, and shall decide questions of order, subject to an appeal to the house. In committee of the whole he shall call some member to the chair, and may debate any question before the committee; in the house he may also call a member to the chair, but such a substitution shall not extend beyond an adjournment. He shall, unless otherwise directed by the house, appoint all committees. He shall vote on a call of the yeas and nays. In the absence of the speaker, the house shall appoint a speaker pro tem.

II. Any ten members may make a call of the house and require absent members to be sent for; but a call of the house cannot be made after the voting has commenced; and the call of the house being ordered, and the absentees noted, the doors shall be closed, and no member permitted to leave the room until the report of the sergeant-at-arms be received and acted upon, or further proceedings in the call be dispensed with by a vote of the majority of the members elect.

III. All questions shall be put in this form : " Those who are of opinion (as the case may be) say aye. Those of a contrary opinion, say no;" and in doubtful cases any member may call for a division.

IV. When a motion is made and seconded, it shall be stated by the speaker, or read by the clerk, previous to debate. If any member require it, all motions (except to adjourn, postpone or commit) shall be reduced to writing. Any motion may be withdrawn by consent of the house before decision or amendment.

V. Every member present, when a question is put or when his name is called, shall vote, unless the house shall, for special cause, excuse him; but it shall not be in order for a member to be excused after the house has commenced voting.

VI. A motion to adjourn shall always be considered in order, and together with a call for the previous question, and a motion to lie on the table shall be decided without debate. But a motion to adjourn shall not be received when the house is voting on another question.

VII. When any member is about to speak in debate, or deliver any matter to the house, he shall arise from his seat, and respectfully address himself to "Mr. Speaker," and shall confine himself to the question under debate and avoid personality.

VIII. When two or more members shall rise at once, the speaker shall name the member who is first to speak.

IX. Whilst the speaker is putting any question, or addressing the house, no member shall walk out nor across the house, or when a member is speaking, shall walk between him and the chair.

X. No member shall speak except in his place, nor more than twice on any question, except on leave of the house.

XI. When a question is under debate, no motion shall be received unless to adjourn, to lie on the table, for the previous question, to postpone to a day certain, to commit, to amend, or to postpone indefinitely ; and these several motions shall have precedence in the order in which they stand arranged. A motion to postpone to a day certain, to commit, or to postpone indefinitely, being decided, shall not be again allowed on the same day, and at the same stage of the bill or proposition. A motion to strike out the enacting words of a bill shall .have precedence of a motion to amend, and if carried, shall be equivalent to the rejection of the bill.

XII. The previous question shall be in this form : " Shall the main question be now put?" It shall only be admitted when demanded by a majority of the members present, and its effects shall be to put an end to all debate, and bring the house to a direct vote upon pending amendments, and then upon the main question. On a motion for the previous question, and prior to the seconding of the same, a call of the house shall be in order; but after a majority shall have seconded such motion, no call shall be in order prior to a decision of the main question.

XIII. Any member may call for a division of the question, hen the same will admit thereof.

XIV. No committee shall absent themselves by reason of their appointment, during the sitting of the house, without special leave, except committees of conference.

XV. Every bill shall be introduced by motion for leave, or by order of the house on a report of the committee. In cases of a general nature, one day's notice at least shall be given of the motion to bring in a bill,

XVI. Every bill shall receive three several readings previous to its passage ; but no bill shall receive its second and third readings on the same day.

XVII. The first reading of a bill shall be for information, and if objections be made to it, the question shall be, " Shall the bill be rejected." If no objection be made, or the question to reject be lost, the bill shall go to its second reading without further question.

XVIII. All bills, resolutions, memorials, &c., requiring the approval of the governor, shall, on the second reading, be considered by the house in committee of the whole, before they shall be taken up and considered by the house. The final question upon the second reading of every bill or other paper originating in the assembly and requiring three readings previous to being passed, shall be, "Shall it be engrossed and read the third time?" and upon every such bill or paper originating in the senate, "shall it be read a third time?" And the question upon every bill or resolution of the senate, that requires three readings, shall be, previous to being passed, "Whether it shall be ordered to a third reading?" No bill or resolution that requires three readings, shall be committed or amended until it shall have been twice read, (12) and all joint resolutions which will require the signature of the governor, shall take the same course as to their reading (14) as in the case of bills, unless otherwise ordered by the house.

XIX. Amendments made in committee of the whole, shall not be read by the speaker on his resuming the chair, unless requested by one or more of the members.

XX. On the third reading of a bill or resolution, no amendment (except to fill blanks) shall be received, except by the unanimous consent of members present.

XXI. A bill or resolution may be re-committed at any time previous to its passage ; if any amendment be reported upon such commitment, the question shall be upon concurring in the amendment, and the question for its engrossment and a third reading may then be put.

XXII. In filling blanks, the largest sum and longest time shall be first put, and when the house is equally divided, in such case the question shall be lost.

XXIII. On Fridays and Saturdays of each week, bills and resolutions which do not elicit debate, shall be considered in their order on the calendar of business in preference to all other business, and this rule shall govern the order of business, when the house is in committee of the whole.

XXIV. When a motion or question has been once made and carried in the affirmative or negative, it shall be in order for any member of the majority, or where the house is equally divided, for any member who voted in the negative to move for a reconsideration thereof, on the same or succeeding day. A motion to reconsider being put and lost, shall not be renewed. A motion to reconsider shall always be in order.

XXV. All acts, addresses and resolutions, shall be signed by the speaker, and all writs, warrants and subpoenas issued by order of the house, shall be under his hand and seal, attested by the clerk.

XXVI. Petitions, memorials, and other papers, addressed to the assembly, shall be presented by any member in his place ; a brief statement of the contents thereof shall be made verbally, and endorsed thereon, together with his name, by the member introducing the same, and shall not be debated or decided on the day of their being first read, unless where the house shall direct otherwise; but shall lie on the table, (to be taken up in the order they were read,) or referred on motion to a committee.

XXVII. It shall be in order for the committee on enrolled bills to report at any time, except when questions are being taken.

XXVIII. After examination and report, each bill shall be certified by the clerk, and by him transmitted to the senate; the day of transmission shall be entered on the journal.

XXIX. No member or officer of the assembly shall be permitted to read newspapers within the bar of the house, while the house is in session, or smoke in the assembly room at any time.

XXX. Any member offering a resolution in the house, may read the same in his place, before sending it to the chair. It shall then be read by the clerk and when so read, shall be considered to be before the house, but it shall not be acted upon by the house on the same day on which it is offered, without leave.

XXXI. It shall be competent for one-sixth of the members present, when a question is taken, to call for the ayes and noes, which shall be recorded by the clerk.

XXXII. No standing rule or order of the house shall be rescinded or changed, without one day's notice being given of the motion therefor. Nor shall any rule be suspended except by a vote of at least two-thirds of the members present. Nor shall the order of business, as established by the rules of the house, be postponed or changed, except by a vote of at least two-thirds of the members present.

XXXIII. All bills and resolutions brought into the house by any member or committee, shall be endorsed by the member or committee bringing in the same.

XXXIV. When a member is called to order, he shall sit down, and shall not speak except in explanation, until the speaker shall have determined whether he is in order or not; and every question of order shall be decided by the speaker, subject to an appeal to the house by any member, and if a member be called to order for words spoken, the exceptionable words shall be taken down in writing, that the speaker and house may be better enabled to judge.

The standing committees of the assembly shall consist of five members each, and be as follows:

1st.   On the Judiciary.
2d.   On Ways and Means.
3d.   On Education, School and University Lands.
4th.   On Incorporations.

5th. On Rail Roads.

6th. On Claims.

7th. On Internal Improvements.

8th. On Roads, Bridges and Ferries.

9th. On Town and County Organization.

10th. On the Militia.

11th. On Privileges and Elections.

12th. On Agriculture and Manufactures.

13th. On the Expiration and Re-enactment of Laws.

14th. On Legislative Expenditures.

15th. On State Affairs.

16th. On Public Printing.

17th. On Contingent Expenditures.

18th. On Engrossed Bills.

19th. On Enrolled Bills.

20th. On State Lands.

21st. On Mining and Smelting.

22d. On Charitable and Religious Societies.

23d. On State Prison.

24th. On Medical Societies and Medical Colleges.

XXXV. The two last readings of all bills appropriating money, shall be at length; and a suspension of this rule shall not be made without the unanimous consent of the house.

XXXVI. The hour for the meeting of the assembly shall be at 10 o'clock, A. M.

XXXVII. Whenever any disturbance or disorderly conduct shall occur in the lobby, the speaker, (or the chairman of the committee of the whole) shall have power to cause the same to be cleared of all persons except members and officers of the house.

XXXVIII. Reporters for newspapers can have seats assigned them by the speaker, within the bar of the chamber, for the purpose of taking down the proceedings, but not so as to interfere with the convenience of the assembly.

14

XXXIX. A clerk shall be elected at the commencement of each session, to hold his office at the pleasure of the house; he shall keep a correct journal of the daily proceedings of the body, and perform such other duties as may be assigned to him; he shall superintend the recording of the journal of proceedings, the engrossing, enrolling, transcribing and copying of bills, resolutions, &c., shall permit no records nor papers belonging to the assembly to be taken out of his custody, otherwise than in the regular course of business; shall report any missing papers to the notice of the speaker; and generally shall perform under the direction of the speaker, all duties pertaining to his office as clerk.

XL. A sergeant-at-arms shall be elected at the commencement of each session, to hold his office at the pleasure of the house. It shall be his duty to execute all orders of the speaker or house, and to perform all duties they may assign to him connected with the police and good order of the assembly chamber—to exercise a supervision over the ingress and egress of all persons to and from the chamber, to see that messages, &c., are promptly executed, that the requisite fires are kept up during the appropriate season, that the hall is properly ventilated, and is open for the use of the members of the assembly from 8 A. M. until 9 o'clock P. M., and to perform all other services pertaining to the post of sergeant-at-arms.

XLI. A majority of all the members elected to the assembly must be present to constitute a quorum for the transaction of business; any ten of their number, however, can adjourn from time to time, and have power to compel the attendance of absent members.

XLII. No member or officer of the assembly, unless from illness or other cause he shall be unable to attend, shall absent himself from the sessions of the assembly during an entire day without first having obtained leave of absence; and no one shall be entitled to draw pay while absent more than one entire day without leave, except he be confined by sickness at the seat of government.

XLIII. Any committee required or entitled to report upon a subject referred to them, may make a majority and minority report; and any member of such committee, dissenting in whole or in part from either the conclusion or the reasoning, of both the majority and minority, shall be entitled to present to the assembly a brief statement of his reasons for such dissent, which, if decorous in its language, and respectful to the assembly, shall be entered at length on the journal in connection with the majority and minority reports.

XLIV. The rules observed in the assembly shall govern as far as practicable the proceedings in committee of the whole; except that a member may speak oftener than twice on the same subject, and that a call for the ayes and noes, or for the previous question, cannot be made in committee.

XLV. Two hundred and forty copies of every bill reported by a standing committee, also of every joint resolution or memorial, shall be printed, after the second reading, unless otherwise ordered. And all bills, resolutions and memorials, that shall be printed, shall remain at least one day on the files, after being printed, before being considered.

XLVI. The rules of parliamentary practice, comprised in Jefferson's Manual, shall govern the assembly in all cases to which they are applicable, and in which they are not inconsistent with these rules, and the orders of the assembly, and the joint rules and orders of the senate and assembly.

Which was adopted.

And also reported the following resolution:

Resolved, That 750 copies of the rules of this house, be printed (under the direction of the speaker,) together with such statistical matter as in his judgment, will be useful to the assembly. 100 of said copies shall be deposited with the librarian, by him to be delivered to the next assembly, and the balance to be distributed in the usual manner.

REGULATIONS FOR THE DAILY TRANSACTION OF BUSINESS.

After the Journal shall have been read, and an opportunity given to correct it, the order of business shall be as follows :

1. Letters, petitions, memorials, remonstrances and accompanying documents may be presented and referred.

2. Resolutions may be offered and considered, notices of leave to introduce bills may be given, and bills may be introduced on leave granted.

3. Reports of committees may be made and considered, first from standing committees, and next from select committees.

4. Messages and other executive communications.

5. Messages from the senate.

6. Bills and resolutions from the senate on their second reading.

7. Bills on their third reading.

8. Bills ready for a third reading.

9. Bills reported by a committee of the whole.

10. Bills in which a committee of the whole has made progress and obtained leave to sit again.

11. Bills not yet considered in committee of the whole.

12. After one hour shall have been devoted to the consideration of business under the first, second and third heads, the assembly shall proceed to dispose of the business on the speaker's table and to the orders of the day.

STANDING COMMITTEES OF THE ASSEMBLY.

JUDICIARY—Messrs. Cate, Sanders, E. Robinson, Barber and Tweedy.

WAYS AND MEANS—Messrs. J. E. Holmes, H. L. Foster, Carlile, Thomas and Bacon.

EDUCATION, SCHOOL AND UNIVERSITY LANDS——Messrs. Wright, McKesson, H. C. West, Bell and Taylor.

INCORPORATIONS—Messrs. C. Reed, Fenton, W. P. Barnes, Pearle and Belden.

RAIL ROADS—Messrs. Dennis, Haertel, C. Reed, Olmstead and Kelsey.

CLAIMS——Messrs. Rogan, Gage, C. B. Coleman, Hill and H. Holmes.

INTERNAL IMPROVEMENTS—Messrs. Wilcox, Miller, Cate, Stebbins and Ostrander.

ROADS, BRIDGES AND FERRIES——Messrs. Resley, Maxson, Lees, Block and Schutte.

TOWN AND COUNTY ORGANIZATION—Messrs. McGarry, Kelsey, Loehr, Powers and Seaver.

MILITIA—Messrs. McKesson, Madden, Roche, Stebbins and Adams.

PRIVILEGES AND ELECTIONS—Messrs. Hillyer, Dodge, Woodman, T. West and Murray.

AGRICULTURE AND MANUFACTURES—Messrs. O. Reed, Sayles, Roe, York and Lauderdale.

EXPIRATION AND RE-ENACTMENT OF LAWS—Messrs. Wheeler, E. N. Foster, Conner, Armstrong and Bacon.

LEGISLATIVE EXPENDITURES—Messrs. Haertel, Simpson, Dennis, Burdick and Hays.

STATE AFFAIRS—Messrs. Ricker, La Due, H. Barnes, Sholes and Taylor.

PUBLIC PRINTING—Messrs. La Due, Wright, Tallmadge, Sholes and Hawkins.

CONTINGENT EXPENDITURES—Messrs. Simpson, Hillyer, J. Robinson, Meyer and Field.

ENGROSSED BILLS—Dodge, H. L. Foster, Kelly, Davis and Bartlett.

ENROLLED BILLS—Chamberlin, Wheeler, Adams, Resley and Block.

STATE LANDS—Tallmadge, O. Reed, Stevens, Fenton and Olmstead.

MINING AND SMELTING—E. Robinson, Madden, York, Sayles and Armstrong.

CHARITABLE AND RELIGIOUS SOCIETIES—H. C. West, J. E. Holmes, Wilcox, Thomas and Seaver.

STATE PRISON—Miller, W. P. Barns, Rogan, Donaldson and Fellows.

MEDICAL SOCIETIES AND MEDICAL COLLEGES—O. D. Coleman, Maxson, Chase, Bartlett and Porter.

FINANCE—Simpson, Sayles, McGarry, Bacon and Taylor.

JOINT RULES AND ORDERS OF THE SENATE AND ASSEMBLY.

1st. In all cases of disagreement between the Senate and Assembly, if either house shall request a conference, and appoint a committee for that purpose, the other house shall appoint a similar committee, and such committee shall, at a convenient hour, to be agreed upon by their chairman, meet in the conference chamber, and state to each other verbally, or in writing, as either shall choose, the reasons of their respective houses for or against the disagreement, and confer freely thereon; and they shall be authorized to report to their respective houses such modification or amendments as they may think advisable.

2d. When a message shall be sent from the Senate to the Assembly, it shall be announced at the door of the Assembly by the Sergeant-at-arms, and shall be respectfully communicated to the chair by the person by whom it may be sent.

3d. The same ceremony shall be observed when a message shall be sent from the Assembly to the Senate.

4th. Messages shall be sent by such persons as a sense of propriety in each house may determine to be proper.

5th. After a bill shall have passed both houses, it shall be duly enrolled by or under the direction of the chief clerk of the Senate, or chief clerk of the Assembly, as the bill may have originated in one or the other house, before it shall be presented to the Governor for his approval.

6th. When a bill is duly enrolled, it shall be examined by a joint committee of five, two from the Senate and three from the Assembly, appointed for that purpose, who shall carefully compare the enrolled with the engrossed bill, as passed in the two houses, and correcting any errors that may be discovered in the enrolled bill and make their report forthwith to the respective houses.

7th. After examination and report, each bill shall be signed in the respective houses, first by the Speaker of the Assembly, then by the President of the Senate.

8th. After a bill shall have been thus signed in each house, it shall be presented by the said committee to the Governor for his approval, it being first endorsed on the back of the roll, certifying in which house the same originated, which endorsement shall be signed by the chief clerk of the Senate or Assembly, as the bill may have originated in the one or the other house, and the said committee shall report the day of presentation to the Governor, which shall be entered on the journal of each house.

9th. All orders, resolutions, and votes which are to be presented to the Governor for his approval, shall also in the same manner be previously enrolled, examined and signed, and then be presented in the same manner, and by the same committee, as is provided in case of bills.

10th. When a bill or resolution, which shall have passed in one house is rejected in the other, notice thereof is to be given to one house in which the same may have passed.

11th. When a bill or resolution, which has been passed in the house, is rejected in the other, it shall not be again brought in during the same session without a notice of five days, and leave of two-thirds of the house in which it shall be renewed.

12th. Each house shall transmit to the other all papers on which any bill or resolution shall be founded.

13th.   After each house shall have adhered to their disagreement, a bill or resolution is lost.

14th.   Whenever any report of a joint committee, or other document, shall be presented to both houses of the legislature, the house first acting on the same, if it shall be thought necessary to have it printed, shall order a sufficient number of copies for both branches, and shall immediately inform the other house of its action upon the subject.

15th.   Neither house shall adjourn during any session thereof, without the consent of the other, for a longer period than three days.

16th.   The committee of each house on state affairs, on enrolled bills, and legislative expenses, shall act jointly.

17th.   When a bill, resolution, or memorial, shall have passed either house, which requires the concurrence of the other, it shall be transmitted to said house without the necessity of entering an order on the journal of the house, in which it passed, requesting the concurrence of the other house.

18th.   It shall be in the power of either house to amend any amendment made by the other, to any bill, memorial, or resolution.

19th.   Whenever there shall be a joint convention of the two houses, the proceedings shall be entered at length on the journal of each house.

POPULATION OF UNITED STATES BY STATES.

Maine	581,763		Alabama	426,515
New Hampshire	317,389		Mississippi	291,536
Vermont	312,756		Louisiana	254,271
Massachusetts	985,498		Texas	133,131
Rhode Island	144,012		Arkansas	162,071
Connecticut	363,189		Tennessee	756,893
New York	3,042,574		Kentucky	770,061
New Jersey	466,240		Missouri	592,077
Pennsylvania	2,258,480		Ohio	1,951,101
Delaware	71,239		Michigan	393,156
Maryland	418,590		Indiana	983,634
Virginia	894,149		Illinois	853,059
North Carolina	552,477		Wisconsin	303,600
South Carolina	274,775		Iowa	191,830
Georgia	513,083		California	200,000
Florida	47,120			
			Total	19,517,885

POPULATION OF TERRITORIES OF UNITED STATES.

District of Columbia	38,027		Terr. of Oregon	20,000
Terr. of Minnesota	6,192		Terr. of Utah	25,000
Terr. of New Mexico	61,632			
			Total	150,851

Total Population of United States 19,517,885

Total Population of Territories of U. S.   150,851

Total United States and Territories   19,668,736

SPEAKERS OF THE ASSEMBLY

FROM ORGANIZATION OF TERRITORY OF WISCONSIN TO JANUARY 1853.

TERRITORY.

Names.	Date of Election.
Peter Hill Angle	October 26th, 1836.
Isaac Liffler	November 10th, 1837.
John W. Blackstone	November 29th, 1838.
Lucius I. Barber	January 23d, 1839.
E. V. Whiton	December 5th, 1839.
Nelson Dewey	August 4th, 1840.
David Newland	December 8th, 1840.
David Newland	December 11th, 1841.
Albert G. Ellis	December 7th, 1842.
George H. Walker	December 5th, 1843.
George H. Walker	January 7th, 1845.
Mason C. Darling	January 5th, 1846.
William Shew	January 5th, 1847.
Timothy Burns	February 7th, 1848.

STATE.

N. E. Whitesides	June 6th, 1848.
Harrison C. Hobart	January 11th, 1849.
Moses M. Strong	January 9th, 1850.
Frederick W. Horn	January 9th, 1851.
J. McM. Shafter	January 15th 1852.
Henry L. Palmer	January 13: 1853.

CLERKS OF THE ASSEMBLY.

Names.	Date of Election.
Warren Lewis	October 26th, 1836.
John Catlin	November 8th, 1837.
John Catlin	November 29th, 1838.
John Catlin	January 22d, 1839.
John Catlin	December 3d, 1839.
John Catlin	August 4th, 1840.
John Catlin	December 8th, 1840.
John Catlin	December 11th, 1841.
John Catlin	December 7th, 1842.
John Catlin	December 5th, 1843.
La Fayette Kellogg	January 8th, 1845.
La Fayette Kellogg	January 6th, 1846.
La Fayette Kellogg	January 5th, 1847.
La Fayette Kellogg	February 8th, 1848.

STATE.

Daniel Noble Johnson . . .	June 6th, 1848.
Robert L. Ream	January 11th, 1849.
Alexander T. Gray	January 9th, 1850.
Alexander T. Gray	January 9th, 1851.
Alexander T. Gray	January 15th, 1852.
Thomas McHugh	January 13th, 1853.

SERGEANTS-AT-ARMS OF THE ASSEMBLY.

TERRITORY.

Names.	Date of Election.
Jesse M. Harrison	October 26th, 1836.
William Morgan	November 8th, 1837.
Thomas Morgan	November 29th, 1838.
Thomas J. Moorman	January 23d, 1839.
James Durley	December 3d, 1839.
D. M. Whitney	August 4th, 1840.
Francis M. Rublee	December 8th, 1840.
Thomas J. Moorman	December 11th, 1841.
William S. Anderson	December 7th, 1842.
John W. Trowbridge	December 5th, 1843.
Chauncey Davis	January 8th, 1845.
David Bonham	January 6th, 1846.
E. R. Hugunin	January 5th, 1847.
John Mullanphy	February 8th, 1848.

STATE.

John Mullanphy	June 6th, 1848.
Felix McLinden	January 11th, 1849.
E. R. Hugunin	January 9th, 1850.
Charles M. Kingsbury	January 9th, 1851.
Elisha Starr	January 15th, 1852.
Richard F. Wilson	January 13th, 1853.

CLERKS IN PUBLIC OFFICES.

———

Charles Geo. Mayers . Deputy Secretary of State . Salary $600.
Daniel M. Seaver . . . Treasurer's Office . . . .   „ $600.
E. A. Calkins . . . . . Superintendent's Office . . .   „ $600.
L. F. Kellogg . . . . . Deputy Clerk of Supreme Court.

SECRETARIES OF STATE.

Thomas McHugh . . . . . . Elected May 1848.
William A. Barstow . . . .   „   Nov. 1849.
Charles D. Robinson . . . .   „   Nov. 1851.

STATE TREASURERS.

J. C. Fairchild . . . . Elected May 1848.
J. C. Fairchild . . . .   „   Nov. 1849.
Edward H. Janssen . . . . .   „   Nov. 1851.

STATE SUPERINTENDENTS OF PUBLIC INSTRUCTION.

Eleazer Root, 2 Terms . . . Elected May 1848.
Azel P. Ladd . . . .   „   Nov. 1851.

STATE ATTORNEYS-GENERAL.

James S. Brown . . . . . . Elected May 1848.
S. Park Coon . . . .   „   Nov. 1849.
Experience Estabrook . . .   „   Nov. 1851.

TERRITORIAL SECRETARIES.

John S. Horner.   Alexander P. Field.
William B. Slaughter.   George R. C. Floyd.
Francis J. Dunn.   John Catlin.

INDEX.

MEMBERS AND OFFICERS OF THE ASSEMBLY.

Names.	RESIDENCE. Town.	County.	Age.	Place of Nativity.	Occupation.	Years in State.	Boarding Place.	Senate District.
John Q. Adams	Fountain Prairie	Columbia	36	Massachusetts	Farmer	9	Badger House	25th
Charles Armstrong	Baraboo	Sauk	39	Ireland	Tailor	5	Waterman	23d
W. D. Bacon	Waukesha	Waukesha	36	New York	Mechanic	11	Varney	10th
J. Allen Barber	Lancaster	Grant	41	Vermont	Lawyer	15	Kellogg	16th
H. Barnes	Middleton	Dane	43	Vermont	Farmer	7	Waterman	11th
W. P. Barns	Newark	Washington	38	New York	Farmer	8	Varney	4th
O. F. Bartlett	East Troy	Walworth	30	New York	Physician	10	Holt	13th
John Bell	Lafayette	Walworth	56	New York	Farmer	8	Severcool	12th
H. E. Block	Potosi	Grant	27	Germany	Merchant	3	American	16th
Philo Belden	Rochester	Racine	36	Connecticut	Farmer	11	Badger House	7th
P. C. Burdick	Albion	Dane	38	New York	Farmer	10	Main	11th
G. W. Cate	Stevens' Point	Portage	29	Vermont	Lawyer	8	Kellogg	2d
Richard Carlile	Milwaukee	Milwaukee	39	England	Printer	8	Mrs. D. Holt	5th
C. E. Chamberlin	Cedarburg	Washington	34	New York	Printer	10	J. T. Wilson	3d
Enoch Chase	Lake Mills	Jefferson	44	Vermont	Farmer	18	Seth Van Bergen	5th
C. B. Coleman	Green Bush	Sheboygan	29	Connecticut	Farmer	6	American	1st
O. D. Coleman	Marcellon	Columbia	31	New York	Physician	4	Miss Howell	25th
Henry Conner	Richwood	Richland	45	Virginia	Farmer	2	N. S. Emmons	15th
J. W. Davis	Fox Lake	Dodge	30	Wales	Lawyer	4½	Varney	22d
William M. Dennis	Emmet	Dodge	40	Rhode Island	Farmer	17	D. Holt	22d
N. M. Donaldson	Waupun	Fond du Lac	41	New York	Farmer	3	American	20th
J. E. Dodge	Waterloo	Grant	42	New York	Farmer	17	American	16th
Thomas Fenton	Mountpleasant	Green	46	Pennsylvania	Farmer	6	Lake House	
T. H. Fellows	Bloomfield	Walworth	40	Pennsylvania	Farmer	13	D. Holt	
S. W. Field	Greenfield	Dane	34	Massachusetts	Farmer	15	J. H. Lewis	
H. L. Foster	Madison	Dane	39	New York	Joiner	14	Home	
E. N. Foster	Mayville	Dodge	42	Massachusetts	Miller	16	Varney	
C. D. Gage	Auburn	Fond du Lac	28	Onondaga, N. Y.	Farmer	6	Madison House	
Titus Hays	Platteville	Grant	34	Ohio	Laborer	7	Mrs. Stark	
R. F. Wilson, Serg't-at-arms	Madison	Dane	27	Maryland	Oakkeeper		American	
W. H. Gleason, Assistant do.	Montello	Marquette	23	New York	Surveyor	2	J. T. Wilson	
F. McLindon, Post Master	Portage City	Columbia		Ireland	Butcher	8	T. Reynolds	
W. L. Smith, Messenger	Madison	Dane		Ohio	Student	10	Home	
J. D. Ballard, do	Madison	Dane		Michigan	Student		Home	
H. Helgerson, Door keeper	Ottaway	Waukesha		Norway	Farmer		Slighten	
Michael Ames F...				Ireland	Farmer		Hotel	

OFFICE

CPSIA information can be obtained
at www.ICGtesting.com
Printed in the USA
BVHW04*1109170918
527708BV00014B/1775/P